---

*About the Marine Sanctuaries Conservation Series*

*The National Oceanic and Atmospheric Administration's National Ocean Service (NOS) administers the Office of National Marine Sanctuaries (ONMS). Its mission is to serve as the trustee for the nation's system of marine protected areas, to conserve, protect, and enhance their biodiversity, ecological integrity and cultural legacy. The existing marine sanctuaries differ widely in their natural and historical resources and include nearshore and open ocean areas ranging in size from less than one to over 5,000 square miles. Protected habitats include rocky coasts, kelp forests, coral reefs, sea grass beds, estuarine habitats, hard and soft bottom habitats, segments of whale migration routes, and shipwrecks.*

*Because of considerable differences in settings, resources, and threats, each marine sanctuary has a tailored management plan. Conservation, education, research, monitoring and enforcement programs vary accordingly. The integration of these programs is fundamental to marine protected area management. The Marine Sanctuaries Conservation Series reflects and supports this integration by providing a forum for publication and discussion of the complex issues currently facing the sanctuary system. Topics of published reports vary substantially and may include descriptions of educational programs, discussions on resource management issues, and results of scientific research and monitoring projects. The series facilitates integration of natural sciences, socioeconomic and cultural sciences, education, and policy development to accomplish the diverse needs of NOAA's resource protection mandate. All publications are available on the Office of National Marine Sanctuaries Web site (http://www.sanctuaries.noaa.gov).*

---

# Climate Impacts to the Nearshore Marine Environment and Coastal Communities: American Samoa and Fagatele Bay National Marine Sanctuary

Edited by Brian Cheng and Emily Gaskin

National Oceanic and Atmospheric Administration
Office of National Marine Sanctuaries
Fagatele Bay National Marine Sanctuary

U.S. Department of Commerce
John Bryson, Secretary

National Ocean and Atmospheric Administration
Jane Lubchenco, Ph.D.
Under Secretary of Commerce for Oceans and Atmosphere

National Ocean Service
David M. Kennedy, Assistant Administrator

Silver Spring, Maryland
August 2011

Office of National Marine Sanctuaries
Daniel J. Basta, Director

## Disclaimer

Report content does not necessarily reflect the views and policies of the Office of National Marine Sanctuaries or the National Oceanic and Atmospheric Administration, nor does the mention of trade names or commercial products constitute endorsement or recommendation for use.

## Report Availability

Electronic copies of this report may be downloaded from the Office of National Marine Sanctuaries web site at http://sanctuaries.noaa.gov. Hard copies may be available from the following address:

National Oceanic and Atmospheric Administration
Office of National Marine Sanctuaries
SSMC4, N/ORM62
1305 East-West Highway
Silver Spring, MD 20910

## Cover

Photo Credits: Oscar Chavez Tafur Mayer, Alexander Churbanov, Claire Fackler, Emily Gaskin,

## Suggested Citation

Cheng, Brian and Emily Gaskin. 2011. Climate Impacts to the Nearshore Marine Environment and Coastal Communities: American Samoa and Fagatele Bay National Marine Sanctuary. Marine Sanctuaries Conservation Series ONMS-11-05. U.S. Department of Commerce, National Oceanic and Atmospheric Administration, Office of National Marine Sanctuaries, Silver Spring, MD. 71 pp.

## Contact

Emily Gaskin
PO Box 4318
Pago Pago, American Samoa
96799, USA
emily.gaskin@noaa.gov
(684) 252-6743

# Abstract

Global and regional changes to the marine environment associated with climate change may have significant consequences for coral reef ecosystems, coastal communities, and maritime heritage resources relevant to the Fagatele Bay National Marine Sanctuary (FBNMS). Regional physical changes to the marine environment include climate variability, sea level rise, ocean circulation patterns, and ocean acidification. These changes combined with anthropogenic stressors may produce cumulative impacts on biodiversity and ecosystem health including changes in physiology, phenology, and population connectivity, and species range shift. This paper identifies and synthesizes potential climate change impacts in American Samoa and the region over the next fifty years. This information will help inform priority management actions for the Sanctuary to take to respond to the impacts of climate change on natural systems and human activities within American Samoa.

# Key Words

Climate Change, Coral Reef Ecosystems, Coastal Communities, Maritime Heritage, Fagatele Bay National Marine Sanctuary, American Samoa

---

# Acknowledgements

The editors would like to thank NOAA's Office of National Marine Sanctuaries for providing funding support toward the coordination of this document, and all of the agencies, organizations, and institutions involved that provided numerous in-kind staff hours toward the completion of this document.

The editors would also like to thank the Influential Scientific Information (ISI) Reviewers who donated their time and expertise as peer reviewers of this document:

Doug Fenner, American Samoa Department of Marine and Wildlife Resources
Melissa Finucane, University of Hawaii, East West Center
Matt Kendall, National Centers for Coastal Ocean Science, NOAA
Britt Parker, Coral Reef Conservation Program, NOAA
Kelley Higgason, Gulf of the Farallones National Marine Sanctuary, NOAA

Finally, the editors would like to acknowledge FBNMS Deputy Superintendent Kevin Grant, as well as NOAA Holling's Scholars Bowen Burditt, Amanda Pruzinsky, and Victoria Szlag, for the time and effort they put into reviewing the document.

---

# Table of Contents

# Authors

**CHAPTER 1**

          *Emily Gaskin*

**CHAPTER 2**

    2.1    *Kelley Anderson*
    2.2    *Kelley Anderson*
    2.3    *Kelley Anderson*
    2.4    *Brian Cheng*

**CHAPTER 3**

          *Kelley Anderson*

**CHAPTER 4**

          *Emily Gaskin*

**CHAPTER 5**

    5.1    *Emily Gaskin, Carolyn Doherty*
    5.2    *Hans Van Tilburg*

**CHAPTER 6**

          *Emily Gaskin*

**CHAPTER 7**

          *Brian Cheng*

# List of Figures

# Acronyms

| | |
|---|---|
| AAIW | Antarctic Intermediate Water |
| ADB | Asian Development Bank |
| CDW | Circumpolar Deep Water |
| CSIRO | Commonwealth Scientific and Industrial Research Organization |
| CRED | Coral Reef Ecosystem Division |
| CLOD | Coralline lethal orange disease |
| DSOW | Denmark Strait Overflow Water |
| DIC | Dissolved inorganic carbon |
| ENSO | El Niño Southern Oscillation |
| EEZ | Exclusive economic zone |
| FBNMS | Fagatele Bay National Marine Sanctuary |
| GAO | Government Accountability Office |
| HSP | Heat shock protein |
| IPCC | Intergovernmental Panel on Climate Change |
| LSW | Labrador Sea Water |
| LIDAR | Light Detection and Ranging |
| MW | Mediterranean Water |
| NCAR | National Center for Atmospheric Research |
| NADW | North Atlantic Deep Water |
| NPGO | North Pacific Gyre Oscillation |
| NPH | North Pacific High |
| NPIW | North Pacific Intermediate Water |
| ONMS | Office of National Marine Sanctuaries |
| PDO | Pacific Decadal Oscillation |
| SST | Sea surface temperatures |
| SPREP | Secretariat of the Pacific Regional Environment Program |
| SECC | South Equatorial Counter Current |
| SEC | South Equatorial Current |
| SPCZ | South Pacific Convergence Zone |
| SPSLCMP | South Pacific Sea Level and Climate Monitoring Project |
| THC | Thermohaline circulation |
| WOCE | World Ocean Circulation Experiment |

# 1.   Introduction

## 1.1.  Purpose of this Document

The primary purpose of *Climate Impacts to the Nearshore Marine Environment and Coastal Communities: American Samoa and Fagatele Bay National Marine Sanctuary* (hereafter referred to as the *Climate Impacts Report*) is to gather and synthesize existing information on the main climate change drivers and the potential consequences for ecosystems, heritage and cultural resources, and local economies relevant to American Samoa and Fagatele Bay National Marine Sanctuary (FBNMS). This document is the precursor and companion to the Climate Change Plan for the sanctuary that will identify priority actions for the sanctuary to take to help address the impacts of climate change specific to the site, its communities, and the region. A Climate Impacts Report and a Climate Change Plan will be developed for all sites in the National Marine Sanctuary System.

The Climate Impacts Report and Climate Change Plan for each site are also being prepared in response to recommendations from a recent Government Accountability Office (GAO) (2007) report on climate change and land and water areas under federal jurisdiction. The report recommended that the Secretary of Commerce (along with the Secretaries for Interior and Agriculture) "develop guidance incorporating agencies' best practices, which advise managers on how to address climate change effects on the resources they manage and gather the information needed to do so."

## 1.2.  Scope of the Document

The *Climate Impacts Report* provides best available information on the potential impacts of climate change to American Samoa and FBNMS. At this time however, there is very limited site specific information available for the sanctuary and the territory. Therefore it was often necessary to draw from regional studies conducted on other island nations in the South Pacific. Wherever possible the authors tried to provide site specific information but when it is not available the scope of the discussion is expanded. Even when the discussion is not specific to American Samoa and FBNMS, the information in this document can still inform priority management actions for the coastal and marine areas in American Samoa. As additional information becomes available, coastal and marine managers should consider adapting their management strategies to reflect new information.

## 1.3.  Problem of Climate Change

Since pre-industrial times, global green house gas emissions have increased dramatically due to human activities. The pre-industrial $CO_2$ concentration was approximately 280 ppm, whereas in the year 2010 it is 388 ppm. For the period between 1970 and 2004, green house gases have increased by 70 percent (Berstein et al. 2007). Consequently, these activities have altered the energy balance of the Earth's climate system. Since 1750, the global average net effect of human activities has been warming as observed by increased air and sea temperatures, widespread melting of snow and ice and rising sea levels. Greenhouse gases alter the climate system in complex ways, influencing patterns of rainfall, storms, and wave activity among others. Additionally, increased atmospheric $CO_2$ concentrations have resulted in direct changes to ocean chemistry (e.g., ocean acidification). However, detecting climate change trends is difficult due to natural variability found in Earth's climate system. Climate can vary over the course of days, months, or thousands of years and can manifest as cycles such as the El Niño Southern Oscillation (ENSO) or the Pacific Decadal Oscillation (PDO).

The effects of green house gas emissions may also be persistent for longer than previously thought. Recent model simulations suggest that a complete cessation of emissions will still result in climate change effects for 1,000 years (Solomon et al. 2009). This is due to slow heat loss by the world's oceans, with the effect of perpetuating climate impacts such as rainfall reductions and sea level rise. Additionally, observed rates of climate change have been greater than projections have realized. For example, observed sea level has been at the uppermost projections by the Intergovernmental Panel on Climate Change (IPCC) Third Assessment Report (Rahmstorf 2007), suggesting that some projections may be underestimating rates of change.

Biological systems in terrestrial and marine habitats have clearly been impacted by climate change. This has manifested in a variety of systems as shifts in species ranges, changes in the timing of important life events (e.g., breeding, migration), and the production of biological "winners" and "losers" that have differing abilities to physiologically adapt to new climate conditions.

## 1.4. Office of National Marine Sanctuaries Program Approach to Climate Change

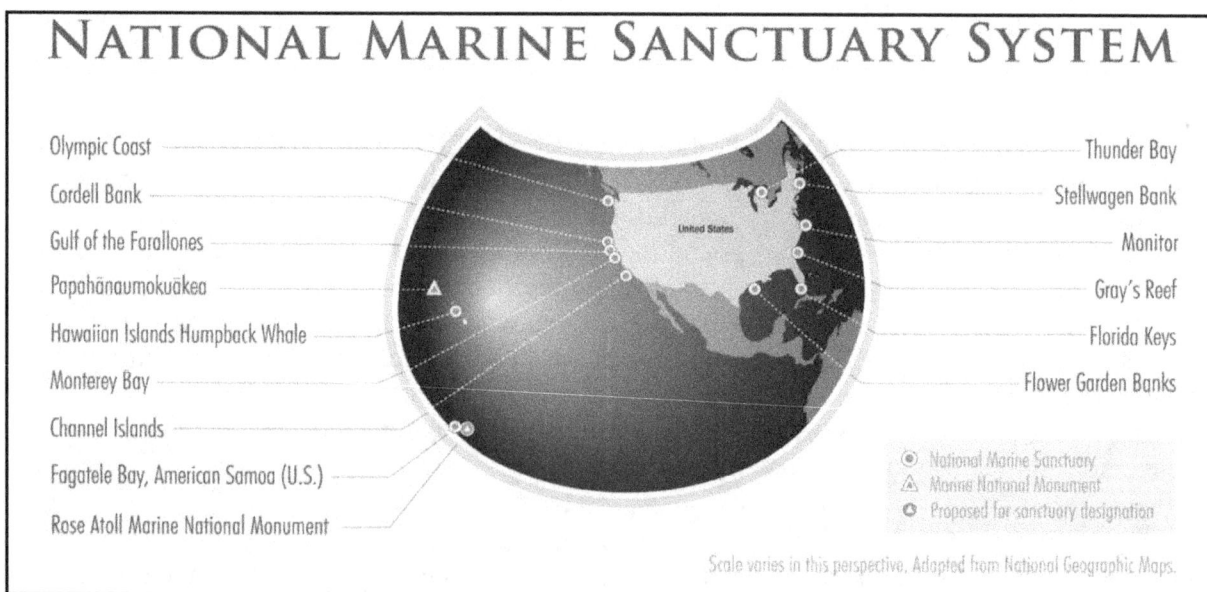

**Figure 1.1.National Marine Sanctuary System. Credit: ONMS.**

The Office of National Marine Sanctuaries (ONMS) recognizes that the science, knowledge, and expertise surrounding climate change are ever evolving and that some problems will be at too large of a scale that the ONMS can directly deal with. Although there will never be a complete suite of information to manage a protected area for climate change impacts, the ONMS has mandated responsibilities for protecting sanctuary resources. Ameliorating existing local and regional stressors and increasing the resilience of local and regional resources will be the most effective management response to climate change. The ONMS must therefore be proactive now;

the price - monetary and otherwise - of being reactive is too high. It is therefore the intent of the ONMS, using the best available science, expertise, tools, and authorities, to manage our sites to minimize, alleviate, and otherwise adapt to the impacts of climate change on sanctuary resources.

## 1.5.  Current Status of Sanctuary Resources

Fagatele Bay National Marine Sanctuary (FBNMS) is a 0.65 sq. km (0.27 sq. mi.) coastal bay formed by a collapsed volcanic crater and includes Fagatele Bay in its entirety (Fig. 1.2). The landward boundary is defined by the mean high high water line between Fagatele Point and Steps Point. The seaward boundary of the sanctuary is defined by a straight line between Fagatele Point and Steps Point. Sanctuary regulations address natural and cultural resource protection, vessel and dive operations, discharge, sea bottom disturbance, use and possession of explosives, poisons or weapons, and damage to sanctuary signs.

**Figure 1.2.Aerial view of Fagatele Bay National Marine Sanctuary. Photo Credit: FBNMS.**

The prevalent feature of Fagatele Bay is its extensive coral reef ecosystem. Shallow-water coral reefs and reef-building organisms are confined to the upper photic zone, with the majority of reef production occurring in less than 30 meters (100 feet) of water. Maximum water depth in the sanctuary is 170 meters (560 feet), with open ocean depths to the southwest dropping off steeply to more than 1,200 meters (4,000 feet). Due to the excellent water and habitat conditions found in the sanctuary, corals are capable of thriving to depths well beyond 30 meters (100 feet).

Fagatele Bay is the smallest and most remote of the National Marine Sanctuaries, but its coral reefs may have the highest marine life diversity in the sanctuary system. The bay's habitats are home to a variety of tropical fish, invertebrates and algae. The coral reefs of the sanctuary provide habitat for at least 271 species of fishes. Surveys have also identified 200 species of coral living on the reefs in the sanctuary. Taxonomic surveys have identified at least 1,400 species of algae and invertebrates (other than coral) living on Tutuila's coral reefs and likely to be found in the sanctuary, and a total of 2,700 species including fish and corals. Mammals, sea turtles, and birds may also be found in or near the sanctuary or surrounding environs. These include several species of dolphins, humpback whales, and hawksbill and green sea turtles.

Imagery and documentation of Fagatele Bay suggests that the sanctuary contains no large submerged archaeological artifacts. However, the site of at least one pre-historic village has been identified and mapped along its shore. This village site is presumed to be a long-occupied fishing village, which exploited the rich resources of the bay. The site consists of foundations of structures and pathways but is currently overgrown by vegetation and has not been excavated.

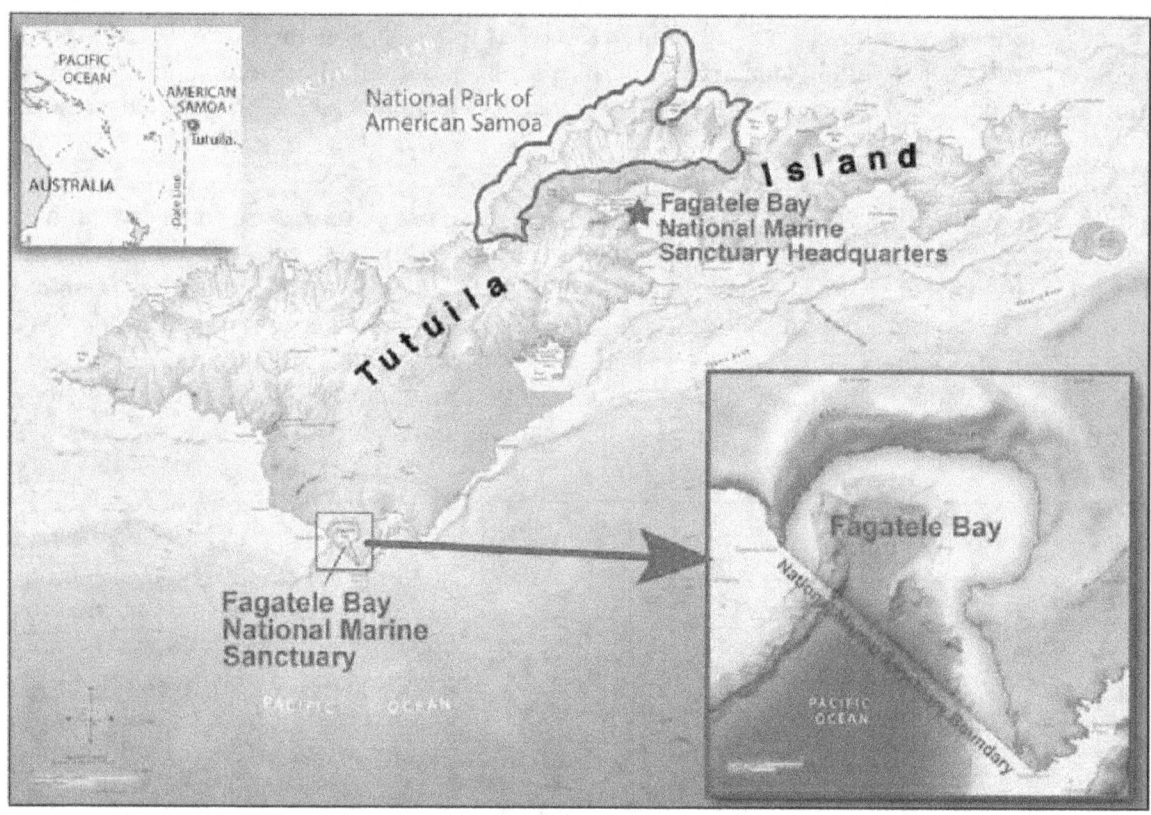

**Figure 1.3.Map of Tutuila Island in American Samoa. Inset map of Fagatele Bay National Marine Sanctuary. Credit: FBNMS.**

## 2.   Main Climate Change Drivers

This chapter explores the primary climate change drivers that are expected to impact Fagatele Bay National Marine Sanctuary (FBNMS) and American Samoa. Variation in weather patterns, including the occurrence of extreme events, is expected under climate change. Detection of these trends is difficult given the natural variability inherent to the Earth's climate system (e.g., El Niño Southern Oscillation [ENSO] and Pacific Decadal Oscillation [PDO]). Rising sea level will also challenge marine organisms that live at the ocean and land interface by potentially modifying inundation times or eroding beach habitat. Changing ocean circulation patterns may modify the delivery of nutrients or the transport of marine larvae critical to population persistence. Finally, this chapter discusses the process of ocean acidification and its potential to radically alter the environmental conditions for marine animals and plants.

### 2.1.  Climate Variation

Variation in weather can have large physical and subsequent biological impacts within the sanctuary. Changing precipitation patterns can affect the extent of freshwater plumes in coastal ecosystems (e.g. lagoons, reefs adjacent bays) as well as the supply of nutrients, sediment and contaminants found in runoff. Tropical cyclones periodically impact the sanctuary as well, with significant wave activity that can overturn and destroy coral colonies. A recurring theme for American Samoa (and globally) is the increased frequency of extreme weather events (Easterling et al. 2000). Frequency for these events can be expressed by calculating the "return period," an estimate for the period of time before a given event will be equaled or exceeded. For a variety of physical factors (e.g. temperature, wind, precipitation), increasing trends are accompanied by increased likelihood of extreme events. In detecting physical patterns of change, it is important to recognize the inherent variation in weather processes that complicates the projection of climate patterns and analysis of trends, further highlighting the need for long-term datasets specific to the region.

### 2.1.1.  Temperature

The IPCC projections suggest that over a broad region, South Pacific Islands (0-S, 150E – 80W55°S, 150°E – 80°W) will experience an average warming of 1.8°C in air temperatures by year 2099, slightly less than global averages (Christensen et al. 2007). Regional analyses of air temperature in Samoa report high variation but suggest a rising trend in maximum air temperatures (Young 2007). For example, using global climate models, the return period of an annual maximum air temperature of 36° C from 1940-1970 was calculated as 5,770 years (Young 2007). In stark contrast, the return period for the same temperature in the year 2100 was 12.4 years.

Local water temperature time series data are much more limited due to a shorter dataset (in operation since 1993). Data is from a Sea Level Fine Resolution Acoustic Measuring Equipment (SEAFRAME) operated by the South Pacific Sea Level and Climate Monitoring Project (SPSLCMP) in Apia, Samoa. The data may not reflect lagoon or open water habitats due to its close proximity to shore (Young 2007). Water temperatures will also be influenced by ENSO.

Satellite measurements from 1981 in the region near Tutuila Island suggest a temperature increase of 0.28°C per 10 years (U.S. EPA 2007) (Fig.2.1). Bleaching events appear to be correlated with sea surface temperatures (SSTs) that approach 30° C. There appears to be some relationship with high SST and ENSO but this relationship is not always consistent (US EPA 2007).

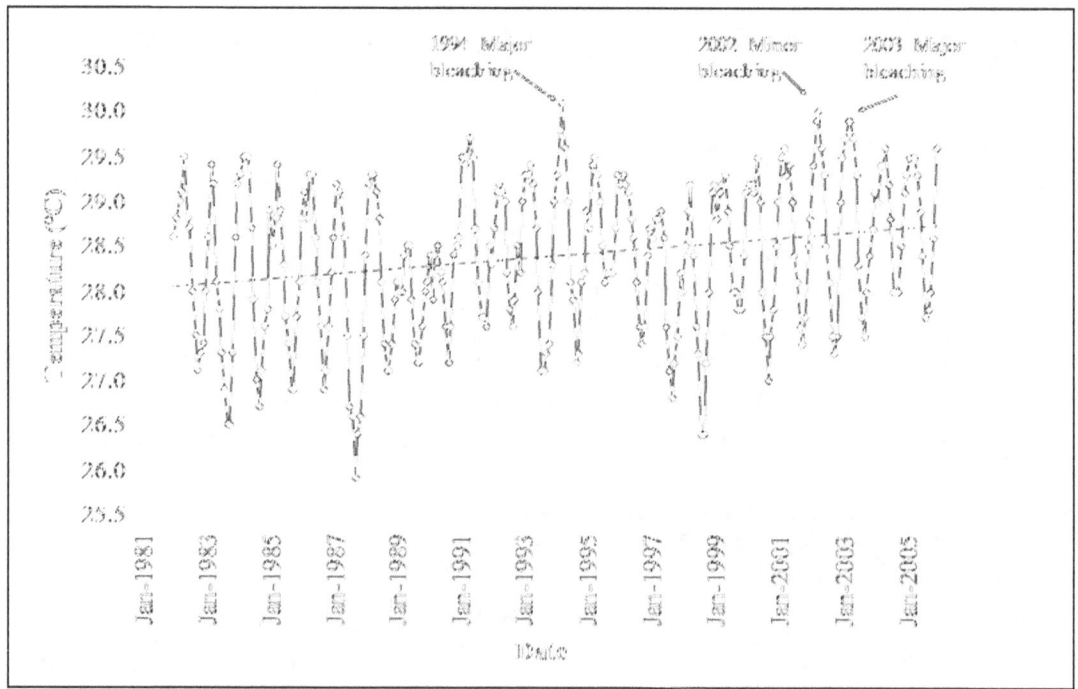

**Figure 2.1.Monthly mean sea surface temperatures in the vicinity of Tutuila Island, American Samoa. Points are monthly means, bars above are maximum mean weekly temperature for the year. Trend-line shows a long term temperature increase for ~0.28°C per 10 years. Credit: Reynolds/National Centers for Environmental Prediction integrated satellite and *in situ* sea surface temperature databases.**

### 2.1.2. Precipitation

Long-term precipitation records from Apia, Samoa from 1890 – 2005 indicate no coherent increasing or decreasing trend in rainfall (Young 2007). As with many other climate variables, when measured on daily, monthly and annual timescales, precipitation exhibits considerable variability. Global climate models were used to explore the effects of increasing greenhouse gases on precipitation using historical records from Apia, Samoa. Using a multi model and climate change emission scenario ensemble, Young (2007) estimated return times for precipitation events of varying magnitudes. Results indicate that extreme events exhibit a decreased return time with ongoing emissions scenarios (Fig. 2.2). In other words, the probability of extreme rainfall events increases with ongoing climate change.

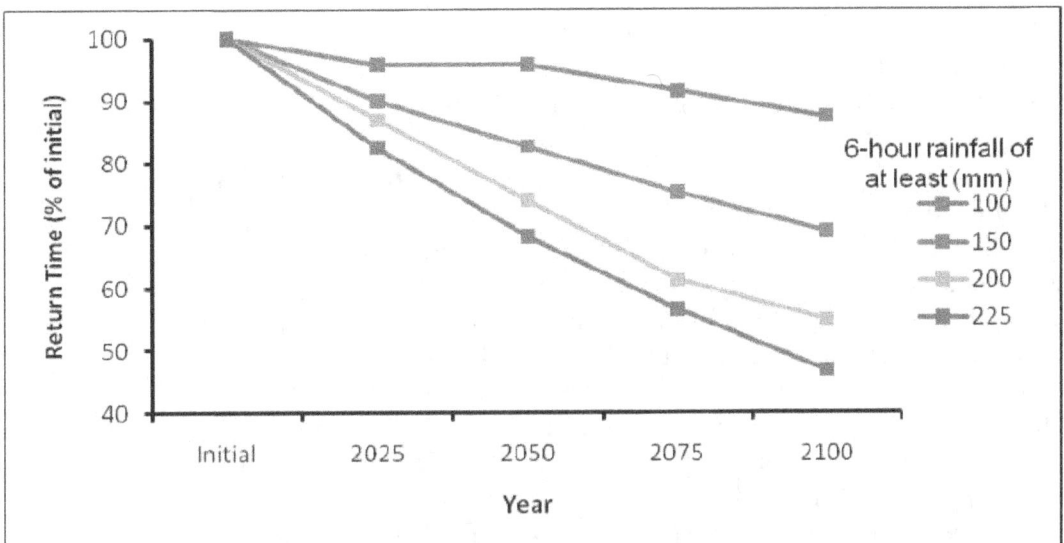

Figure 2.2. This plot graphs return time estimates (as a function of percent of initial return time) over time. The return time refers to the number of years a specified event is statistically likely to occur in. Initial return times are: 100 mm- 2.4 years, 150 mm-8.1 years, 200 mm- 31 years, 225 mm- 63 years. By year 2100, a 225 mm rainfall event is likely to occur once every 29.5 years instead of every 63 years (46.8% of the initial prediction). Credit: Young (2007).

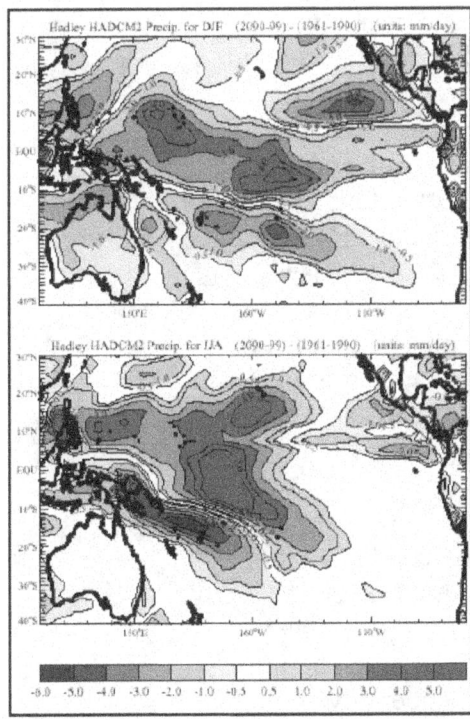

Figure 2.3.Projected changes in total precipitation change for 2090-2099 (for DJF and JJA), color bar in units of mm per day. Credit: East-West Center (2007).

Drought projections were conducted using Canadian global climate models, defined by rainfall conditions less than the 10th percentile (Young 2007). Under this model, high variability in the drought frequency was projected with no long-term trend. A slightly different projection, also using the Canadian global climate models along with IPCC A2 and B2 emissions scenarios, reveals increased incidence of drought under the B2 scenario in the second half of the 21st century. It should be noted that this model was somewhat insensitive to ENSO conditions.

An alternate analysis of rainfall patterns in American Samoa projected declining precipitation in both the winter and summer months (CRAG 2007). However, the model projects American Samoa to be at the intersection of a region of declining precipitation and increased precipitation, suggesting that rainfall projections should be used with caution (Fig. 2.3).

### 2.1.3. El Niño Southern Oscillation

The ENSO is a periodic climate phenomenon that occurs every 3-7 years (Rasmussen and Wallace 1983). The warming phase or "El Niño" is characterized by anomalously warm seawater temperatures in the eastern Pacific Ocean and high surface pressure in the western Pacific. The cool phase or "La Niña" exhibits an opposing pattern of surface pressure and seawater temperature.

The interaction between climate change and ENSO is not well understood and initial studies were not able to discern climate change impacts on the amplitude of ENSO events (van Oldenborgh et al. 2005). Recent work has documented the emergence of a new El Niño signature that exhibits significant trends with ongoing anthropogenic climate change (Yeh et al. 2009). The central Pacific El Niño (CP-El Niño; also referred to as the dateline El Niño and El Niño Modoki) refers to conditions of warm sea surface temperatures in the central Pacific flanked by cooler sea surface temperatures to the west and east (Yeh et al. 2009). This is in contrast to the EP-El Niño, which exhibits the classical warming in the eastern Pacific. Under global warming, the occurrence of CP-El Niño is projected to increase as much as five times (Yeh et al. 2009). The effect of increased incidence of CP-El Niño is not fully understood but would result in greater SST in the central Pacific region accompanied by a westerly shift in rainfall trends (Larkin and Harrison 2005; Yeh et al. 2009).

### 2.1.4. Tropical Cyclones

Since the 1970s, global cyclone destructiveness has increased in the western north Pacific and north Atlantic (Emanuel 2005), resulting in increased peak wind velocities (5-10%) and precipitation (20-30%). Because small increases in wind speed disproportionately increase the destructive power of a cyclone (destructive power increases with wind speed), more recent cyclones have exhibited approximately double the destructive force than earlier cyclones (Emanuel 2005). Between the periods of 1975-1989 and 1990-2004, there was a doubling of category 4 and 5 hurricanes despite small declines in overall cyclone frequency (Webster et al. 2005). Increasing cyclone destructiveness has been attributed to increased cyclone duration and intensity (Emanuel 2005). This is opposed to studies concluding that *overall cyclone frequency* has remained the same (Landsea et al. 1996) or decreased (Emanuel 2008). In addition, El Niño events appear to be linked to the incidence of tropical cyclones in the south Pacific (east of 160°E) (Levinson 2005).

Specific cyclone analyses are lacking for the Samoan region. However, the Samoan exclusive economic zone lies along the eastern edge of a region conducive to development of cyclonic storms in the south Pacific (Craig 2009). Six cyclones have struck or passed near the Samoan Archipelago in the past 30 years including two recent and very powerful Category 5 storms with sustained winds over 155 mph (hurricane Heta in 2004 and hurricane Olaf in 2005). Even infrequent cyclonic storms can have a major impact on coral reef communities. With increasing sea surface temperatures, there is greater energy available to feed these cyclonic storms, increasing their detrimental impact. These storms also bring increased sedimentation and nutrients into the reefs, which can smother and kill coral as well as fuel algal blooms.

### 2.1.5. Winds

Trade winds dominate the atmospheric circulation in the Samoan Archipelago, blowing from northeast to southwest (Pirhalla et al. 2010). Trade winds in American Samoa are typically stronger in the austral winter (June to November) than in the austral summer (Merrill 1989). The South Pacific Convergence Zone (SPCZ) has a major impact on the climate of American Samoa; to the north of the SPCZ winds are generally southwestward while to the south of the SPCZ winds are generally westward (Pirhalla et al. 2010). This convergence results in heightened rainfall, especially during austral summer months (December-February). The SPCZ undergoes shifts in position and intensity on both a seasonal and interannual basis (Pirhalla et al. 2010).

Few wind velocity datasets are available, making the determination of long-term trends difficult. However, global climate models in combination with emissions scenarios suggest that more extreme wind events are likely (Young 2007). This is in part due to intensification of tropical cyclone activity in the region as discussed above. Recent analysis of wind data from 1991-2008 suggest that there has been an increase in the average and 90th percentile of wind speed (Young et al. 2011).

### 2.2. Sea Level Rise

Rising sea levels will have large consequences for marine animals and plants that live at the interface of land and the ocean. Intertidal organisms will have to cope with increased inundation times that may pose greater physiological demands or risk greater exposure to predators. Shore based animals and plants may potentially face decreased coastal habitat due to erosion of beaches as well and/or increased salt intrusion of soils and groundwater. Rising sea levels may also alter water quality properties of nearshore habitats (Ogston and Field 2010), such as nearshore reefs, lagoons and back reef pools that are subject to water circulation patterns that are tied to bathymetry.

### 2.2.1. Observed Trends

Many factors affect local sea level, but two primary factors are linked to climate change: ice melt and thermal expansion of seawater. Of these, ice melt was thought to be the predominant contributor. However, according to the IPCC's 4th Assessment Report (2007), during recent years (1993–2003), for which the observation system has greatly improved, thermal expansion and melting of land ice each account for about half of the observed sea level rise, although there is some uncertainty in the estimates (Solomon et al. 2007). Estimates for the 20th century show that global average sea level rose at a rate of about 1.7 mm per year (Solomon et al. 2007). Satellite observations available since the early 1990s provide more accurate sea level data with nearly global coverage. This decade-long satellite altimetry data set shows that since 1993, sea level has been rising at a rate of around 3 mm per year, significantly higher than the average during the previous half century (Solomon et al.

2007) (Fig. 2.4). Church and White (2006) reconstructed global mean sea level and found that from January 1870 to December 2004, the total global mean sea level rise was 195 mm, an average of 1.44 mm per year. Coastal tide gauge measurements confirm this observation and indicate that similar rates have occurred in earlier decades.

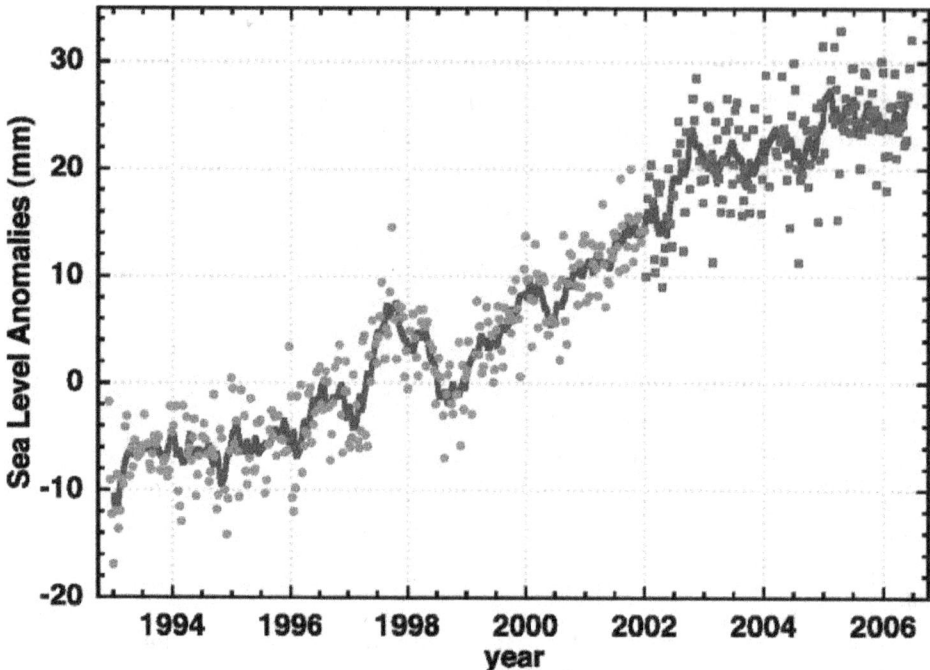

**Figure 2.4.** **Variations in global mean sea level (difference to the mean 1993 to mid-2001) computed from satellite altimetry from January 1993 to October 2005, averaged over 65°S to 65°N. Dots are 10-day estimates (from the TOPEX/Poseidon satellite in red and from the Jason satellite in green). The blue solid curve corresponds to 60-day smoothing. Credit: Cazenave and Nerem (2004) and Leuliette et al. (2004) in Solomon et al. (2007).**

The global coverage of satellite altimetry provides unambiguous evidence of non-uniform sea level change in open oceans; with some regions exhibiting rates of sea level change about five times the global mean (Fig. 2.5). For the past decade, sea level rise shows the highest magnitude in the western Pacific and eastern Indian oceans, regions that exhibit large interannual variability associated with ENSO. These spatial patterns likely reflect decadal fluctuations rather than long-term trends. Analyses of altimetry-based sea level maps over 1993 to 2003 show a strong influence of the 1997–1998 El Niño, with the geographical patterns of the dominant mode being very similar to those of the sea level trend map (e.g. Nerem et al. 1999).

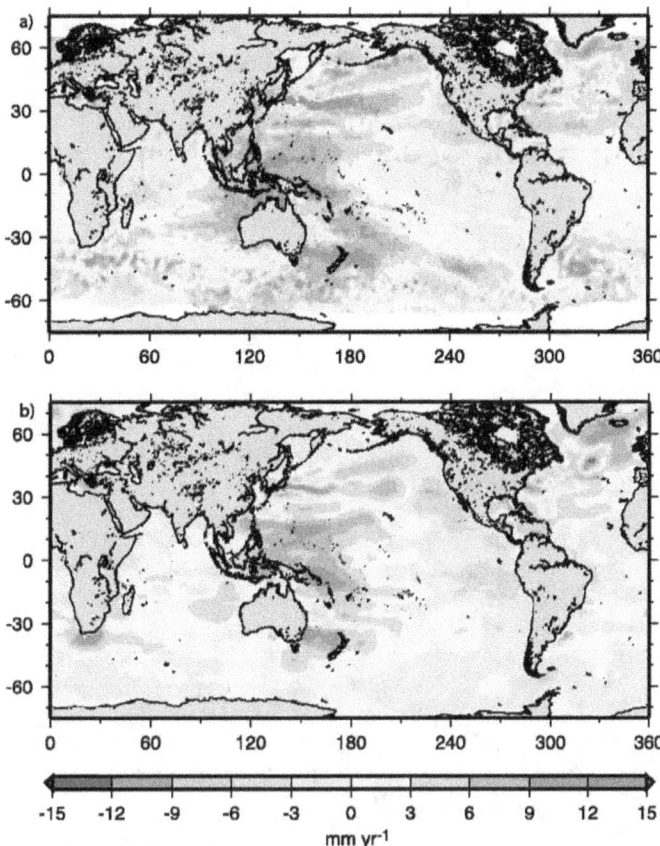

**Figure 2.5. (a) Geographic distribution of short-term linear trends in mean sea level (mm per year) for 1993 to 2003 based on TOPEX/Poseidon satellite altimetry (updated from Cazenave and Nerem, 2004) and (b) geographic distribution of linear trends in thermal expansion (mm per year) for 1993 to 2003. Credit: Ishii et al., (2006) in Solomon et al. (2007).**

The Pacific Ocean region is the center of the greatest interannual variability of the climate system, due to the coupled ocean-atmosphere ENSO (Solomon et al. 2007). Unfortunately, there are few Pacific Island sea level records extending back before 1950. Mitchell et al. (2001) calculated rates of relative sea level rise for the stations in the Pacific region; by taking the records from stations having data for >50 years (five stations) and calculating the average trend over this period, they arrived at a figure of positive relative sea level rise of 1.07 mm per year. Stations having data over periods greater than 25 years (27 stations), the mean trend is positive again but has been reduced to 0.8 mm per year. Solomon et al. (2007) analyzed the station data in Mitchell et al. (2001) of those with more than 50 years of data (4 locations), and found the average rate of sea level rise (relative to the Earth's crust) to be 1.6 mm per year.

The mean sea level rise trend in American Samoa was +2.07 mm per year from 1948 to 2006, (95% confidence interval of $\pm$ 0.90 mm per year) based on monthly mean sea level data, equivalent to an increase of 20.7 cm over 100 years (NOAA Tides and Currents 2010) (Fig. 2.6, Fig. 2.7). Data collected from the SEAFRAME station during 1993-2007 show an increase in mean sea level, at a higher rate (4.9 mm per year); although a longer time series of data is needed to establish a more reliable

11

estimate at this site (SPSLCMP 2007). This is in part because inter-annual fluctuations in sea level are heavily influenced by ENSO events (Alory and Delcroix 1999) (Fig. 2.7).

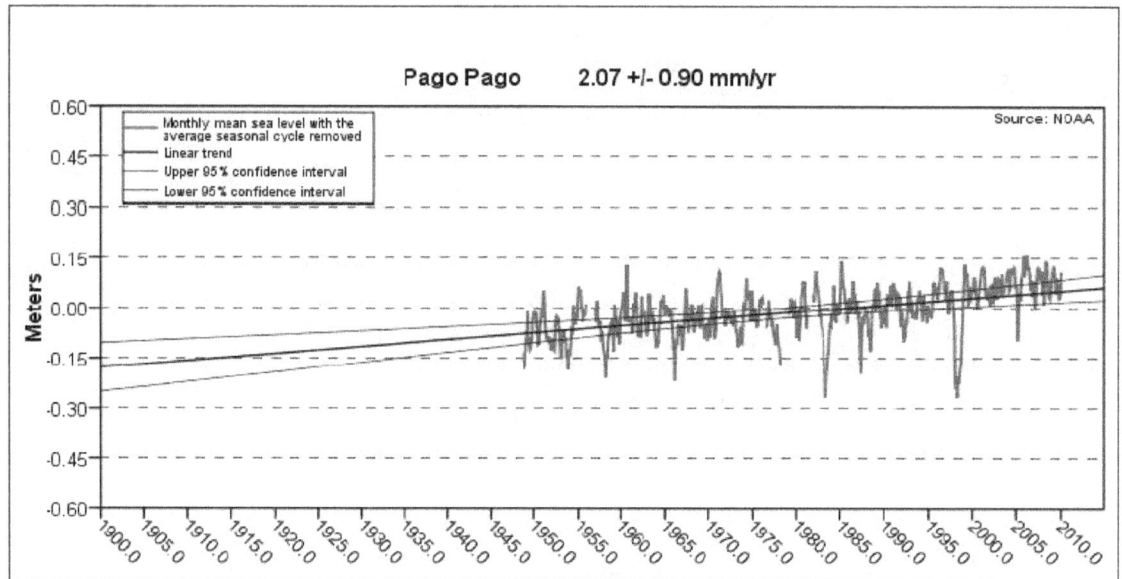

**Figure 2.6. Sea level trends for Pago Pago, American Samoa from 1948 to 2006. Values are monthly averages. The mean sea level trend is 2.07 mm per year with a confidence interval of ±0.90 mm per year. Credit: NOAA Tides and Currents (2010).**

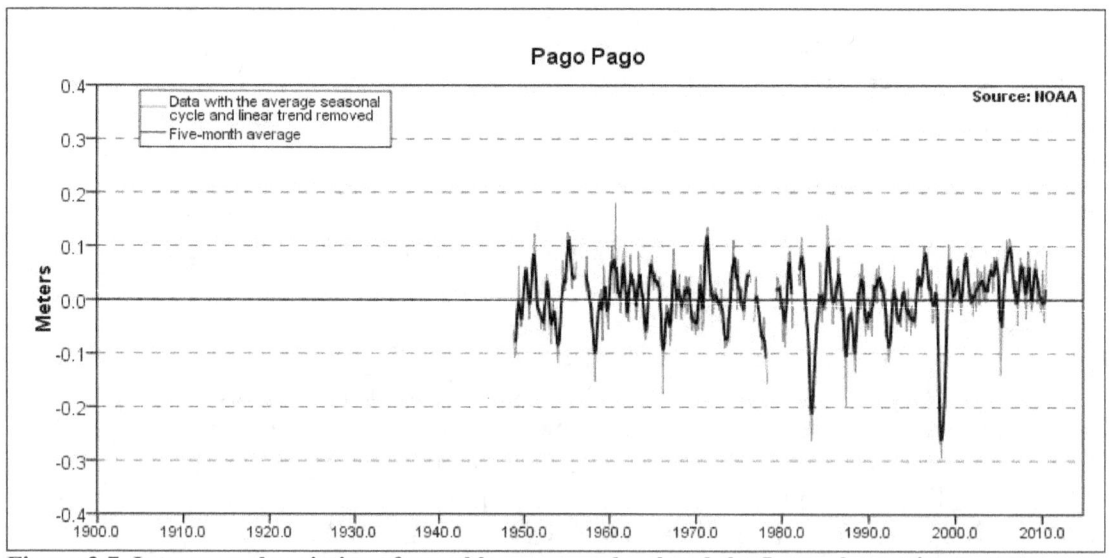

**Figure 2.7. Interannual variation of monthly mean sea level and the 5-month running average. Interannual variation is caused by irregular fluctuations in coastal ocean temperatures, salinities, winds, atmospheric pressures, and ocean currents. The interannual variation for many Pacific stations is closely related to the El Niño Southern Oscillation. Credit: NOAA Tides and Currents (2010).**

### 2.2.2. Projections

While there is quite a range of projections for sea level rise, most model a rise of 1-2 m by the year 2100. The World Health Organization (WHO) project sea level rise of 3.8 mm per year for Samoa, which is higher than global projections of 0.88 – 0.90 m by 2100 (WHO 2010). More recent studies project a global rise of 0.8 – 2.0 m by 2100 (Pfeffer et al. 2008). Numerous papers on the altimetry results (for review see Cazenave and Nerem 2004) show a current rate of sea level rise of $3.1 \pm 0.7$ mm per year over 1993 to 2003 (Cazenave and Nerem 2004; Leuliette et al. 2004) (Fig. 2.8).

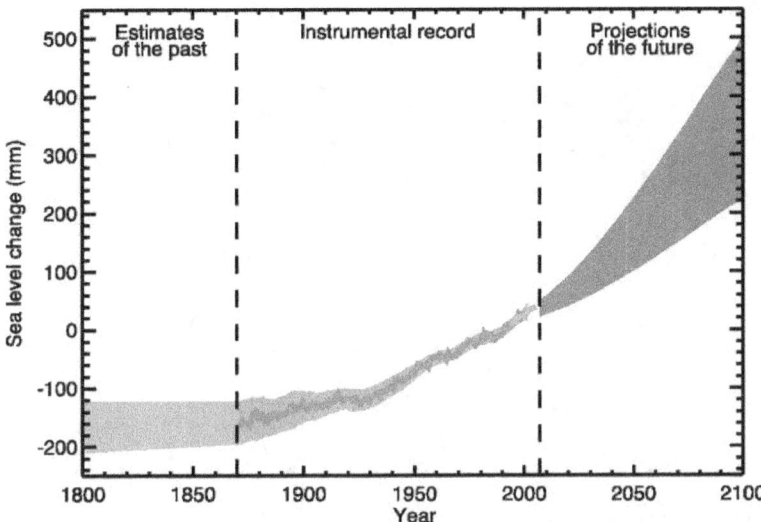

**Figure 2.8. Time series of global mean sea level (deviation from the 1980-1999 mean) in the past and as projected for the future. For the period before 1870, global measurements of sea level are not available. The grey shading shows the uncertainty in the estimated long-term rate of sea level change. The red line is a reconstruction of global mean sea level from tide gauges, and the red shading denotes the range of variations from a smooth curve. The green line shows global mean sea level observed from satellite altimetry. The blue shading represents the range of model projections for the SRES A1B scenario for the 21st century, relative to the 1980 to 1999 mean, and has been calculated independently from the observations. Beyond 2100, the projections are increasingly dependent on the emissions scenario Over many centuries or millennia, sea level could rise by several meters. Credit: Solomon et al. (2007).**

Unfortunately, American Samoa lacks appropriate data (coastal maps, elevation, etc.) to produce robust local sea level rise projections, which is a common problem in the Pacific (Barnett 2001). However, there is currently a study underway conducted by the University of Hawaii's geology department, led by Dr. Chip Fletcher, that aims to yield better projections and inundation maps. Initial steps have been taken in the process of measuring shoreline profiles to gather elevation data, and there are plans of obtaining Light Detection and Ranging (LIDAR) data within a few years. Lacking sea level rise inundation maps, American Samoa currently has no territory-wide sea level rise response plan. Much of American Samoa's population lives on the low-lying plains, making them increasingly vulnerable to flooding, particularly during storms.

## 2.3. Ocean Circulation

The movement of ocean water affects virtually all biological organisms that reside within it by altering the physical properties required for life. These properties range from temperature and salinity to nutrients required for primary production. In marine systems, ocean circulation patterns also influence the spread of larvae produced by a majority of marine organisms, and have large effects on the persistence of populations as well as colonization of new habitat. Unfortunately, climate change impacts on oceanic circulation at a smaller scale are very difficult to predict, particularly where there is limited data on current circulation conditions, such as in American Samoa.

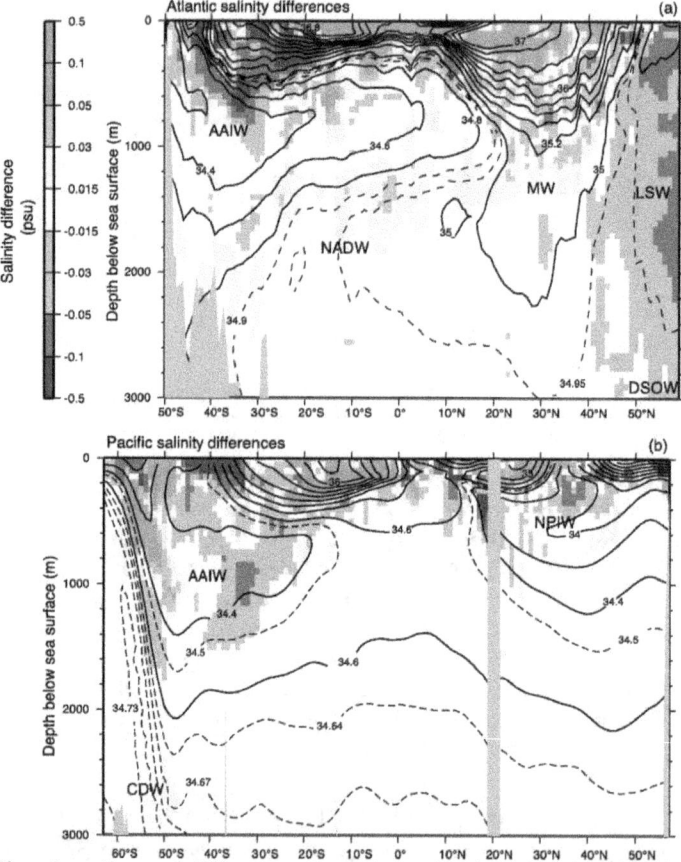

**Figure 2.9.** **Meridional sections of differences in salinity (psu) of the a) Atlantic Ocean for the period 1985 to 1999 minus 1955 to 1969 and b) Pacific Ocean for the World Ocean Circulation Experiment (WOCE) 150°W section (1991–1992) and historical data from 1968 plus or minus 7.5 years. Contours are the mean salinity fields along each section and show the key features. The salinity differences are differences along isopycnals that have been mapped to pressure surfaces. The Atlantic section is along the western side of the Atlantic Ocean and the Pacific section is along 150°W. The two figures are redrafted from Curry et al. (2003) and Wong et al. (2001). Water masses shown include Antarctic Intermediate Water (AAIW), Circumpolar Deep Water (CDW), North Atlantic Deep Water (NADW), Mediterranean Water (MW), Labrador Sea Water (LSW), Denmark Strait Overflow Water (DSOW) and North Pacific Intermediate Water NPIW). The areas shaded in grey represent the seafloor and oceanic crust. Credit: http://www.ipcc.ch/publications_and_data/ar4/wg1/en/ch5s5-3.html in Solomon et al. (2007).**

Surface currents are primarily driven by wind, whereas deep water circulation (> 400 m) is primarily driven by density, a function of temperature and salinity (colder and more saline water is more dense than warm fresh water). Large-scale changes in heat content and salinity have been observed (Solomon et al. 2007) (Fig. 2.9). The IPCC reported that observed changes in salinity are of global scale, with different ocean basins having similar patterns. From the period of the 1960s to the 1990s subtropical waters have increased in salinity and the subpolar surface and intermediate waters have freshened in both the Atlantic and Pacific Oceans in both hemispheres of each ocean (Solomon et al. 2007). These changes in salinity and heat content will result in altered circulation patterns; however the manner in which circulation will be altered remains to be seen.

## 2.3.1. Stratification

Stratification refers to the degree by which seawater density changes with depth. Highly stratified waters are typically characterized by warm or fresh water that resides at the surface and cold or more saline waters at depth. Differences in density therefore create a "barrier" to vertical flux, potentially limiting the vertical transport of the nutrients typically found in deeper water (where they cannot be utilized by biological organisms). The alteration of rainfall amount and spatial and temporal patterns due to climate change can result in small scale alterations of the salinity of near shore water and modify the degree of water column stratification. Small- scale salinity changes in combination with large- scale ocean warming may result in increased stratification, thus reducing mixing and subsequently altering nutrient dynamics. Reduced mixing may extend the periods of time in which near shore reefs persist in higher temperature and hypersaline conditions with cooler freshwater from rainfall floating on top. In the Pacific Ocean, increased stratification could increase the frequency of ENSO events and more extreme climatic variations (Timmermann et al. 1999).

## 2.3.2. Thermohaline Circulation

Thermohaline circulation (THC), also referred to as the great ocean conveyor, is a large-scale ocean circulation pattern that is caused by differences in seawater density (Fig. 2.10). Cooling and ice formation near the poles results in the formation of high density "deep" water that sinks to depth, driving THC. There is much debate over the effects of global climate change on this circulation feature, where a primary concern is a lessening of THC that could result in a cooling of climate over northern Europe (Hansen et al. 2004). Many global climate change models suggest a weakening and possibly complete breakdown of thermohaline circulation, particularly in the Atlantic Ocean (Bernal 1993; Manabe et al. 1994; Sarmiento et al. 1998; Plattner et al. 2001; Vellinga and Wood 2002). In contrast, other models find land-sea interactions result in no change in thermohaline circulation over the 21st century (Latif et al. 2000; Gent 2001).

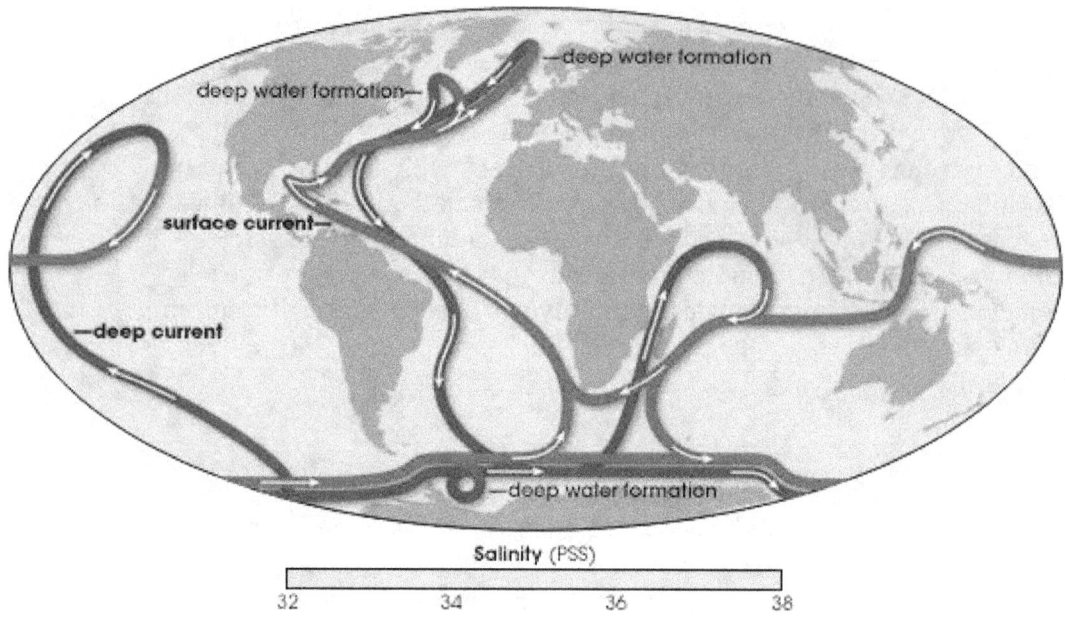

**Figure 2.10**. **Thermohaline circulation (THC) is a global ocean circulation system that is driven by the formation of high density deep water in the North Atlantic and Southern Oceans. Credit: NASA.**

### 2.3.3.  Local Current Patterns

The northern edge of the South Pacific Gyre, which has a counter-clockwise flow, abuts the Samoan archipelago from the southern side (Alory and Delcroix 1999; Tomczak and Godfrey 2003; McClain et al. 2004; Craig 2009). The two surface currents impacting the archipelago are the westward flowing South Equatorial Current (SEC), and the eastward flowing South Equatorial Counter Current (SECC) (Qiu and Chen 2004; Pirhalla et al. 2010). Current intensity is seasonally variable; from March-May the SECC is the dominant current, flowing eastward from about 7-8 ° S to 12-13 ° S with the strongest flow typically in northern American Samoa, near Swains Island (Chen and Qiu 2004; Domokos et al. 2007; Pirhalla et al. 2010). Flowing in the opposite direction, the SEC flows along the north and south sides of the SECC causing current shear and eddy formation (Pirhalla et al. 2010). Location and speed of the currents vary between years. The South Tropical Counter Current generally lies south and west of American Samoa's exclusive economic zone (EEZ), however its influence on circulation is less understood (Qiu and Chen 2004; Pirhalla et al. 2010).

### 2.4.  Ocean Acidification

Increased atmospheric carbon dioxide levels have resulted in ocean acidification, a term that describes the general decrease in pH and alteration to the chemical balance of the ocean. Ocean acidification affects a variety of processes in marine organisms. Most studied has been the effect of acidification on calcification in corals and invertebrates. This is of great importance because calcifying organisms are ubiquitous, with calcifying representatives found in the crustaceans, mollusks, echinoderms and corals, among many others. Ocean acidification may also influence other physiological processes such as sensory capabilities as well as the ability to cope with other stressors such as temperature increases.

The accumulation of atmospheric $CO_2$ due to anthropogenic activities has increased concentrations of seawater carbon dioxide ($CO_2$) and bicarbonate ($HCO_3^-$). Linked to this change in seawater carbon chemistry is a decrease in ocean pH; an observed drop of roughly 0.1 units from pre-industrial levels (Caldeira and Wickett 2003; Orr et al. 2005; Bindoff et al. 2007). If anthropogenic $CO_2$ emissions continue unabated, ocean pH could drop by an additional 0.6 units, a level lower than has occurred in the past 300 million years (Caldeira and Wickett 2003; Meehi et al. 2007). In this scenario, tropical regions and, northern and southern oceans are predicted to be impacted most severely (Orr et al. 2005; Raven et al. 2005).

An increase of $CO_2$ in the atmosphere ($CO_{2atm}$) results in a reduction of ocean pH due to a decline in the carbonate ion concentration ($CO_3^{2-}$) (Caldeira and Wickett 2003). The oceanic carbonate system is controlled by the relative proportions of three forms of dissolved inorganic carbon (DIC) that affect seawater pH as follows:

$$CO_{2atm} \longleftrightarrow CO_{2aq} + H_2O \longleftrightarrow H_2CO_3 \longleftrightarrow H^+ + HCO_3^- \longleftrightarrow 2H^+ + CO_3^{2-}$$

Atmospheric $CO_2$ exchanges across the air-sea interface until equilibrium is reached with aqueous $CO_2$ (Fig. 2.11). The dissolved aqueous $CO_2$ reacts with seawater to form carbonic acid ($H_2CO_3$). Carbonic acid readily dissociates to hydrogen ($H^+$), bicarbonate ($HCO_3^-$), and carbonate ($CO_3^{2-}$) ions (as shown in the equation above). Rising atmospheric $CO_2$ concentrations cause an increase in carbonic acid, a weak acid, resulting in increased hydrogen ion concentrations, leading to a decrease in pH (Fig. 2.12), and reduced carbonate ion concentrations.

The relative effect of ocean acidification on calcifying organisms can be assessed by calculating the "saturation state" of ocean water. The saturation state represents the relative solubility of a mineral such as calcium carbonate and is given as $\Omega$. A lower saturation state reflects increased solubility of the mineral whereas an increased saturation state reflects decreased solubility. High saturation state waters allow for the production of calcium carbonate material by biological organisms. Feely et al. (2004) demonstrate that zones of low saturation state waters are expanding.

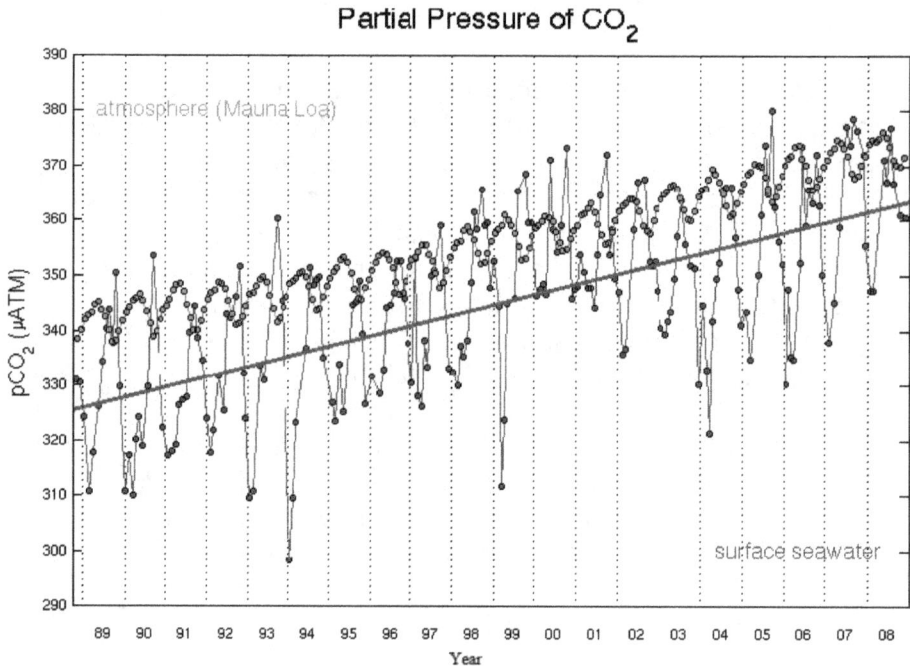

**Figure 2.11.** Changes through time in surface oceanic pCO₂ (in blue) and atmospheric pCO₂ in Mauna Loa, HI Credit: Hawaii Ocean Timeseries (2009).
http://hahana.soest hawaii.edu/hot/trends/trends html

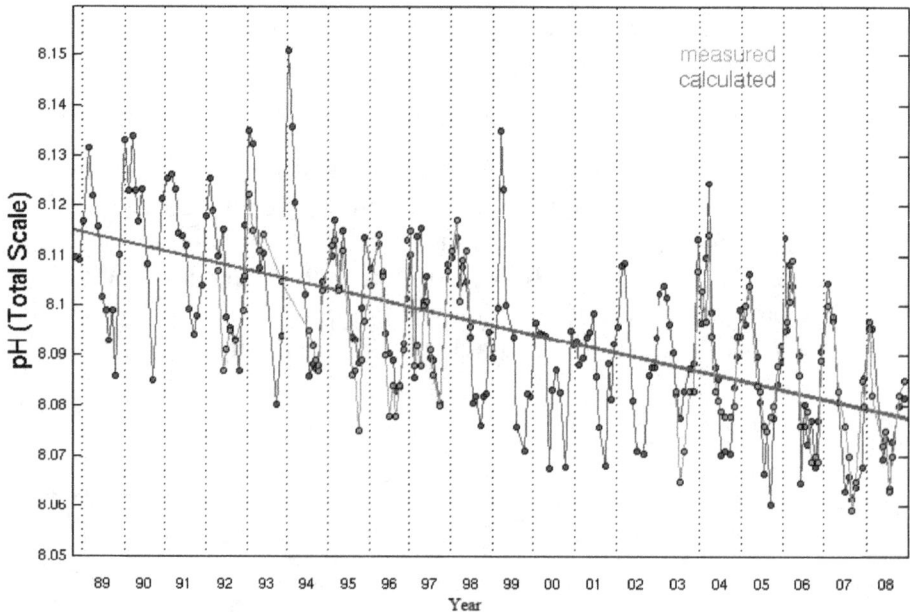

**Figure 2.12.** Changes through time of oceanic pH at HOT's ALOHA station, approximately 65nm north of Oahu, Hawaii. Credit: Hawaii Ocean Timeseries (2009).
http://hahana.soest hawaii.edu/hot/trends/trends html ).

In their Fourth Assessment Report, the IPCC documents that the three stations having the longest time series, all in the northern subtropics, show the partial pressure of $CO_2$ ($pCO_2$) increasing at a rate between 1.6 and 1.9 µatm per year (Fig. 2.13), which was indistinguishable from the atmospheric increase of 1.5 to 1.9 µatm per year. Others have calculated the global average pH decrease to be 0.1 pH units below pre-industrial levels, a change of approximately 26% (Caldeira and Wickett 2003; Orr et al. 2005). A decrease in ocean pH of 0.1 units corresponds to a 30 percent increase in the concentration of $H^+$ in seawater, assuming that alkalinity and temperature remain constant (Solomon et al. 2007).

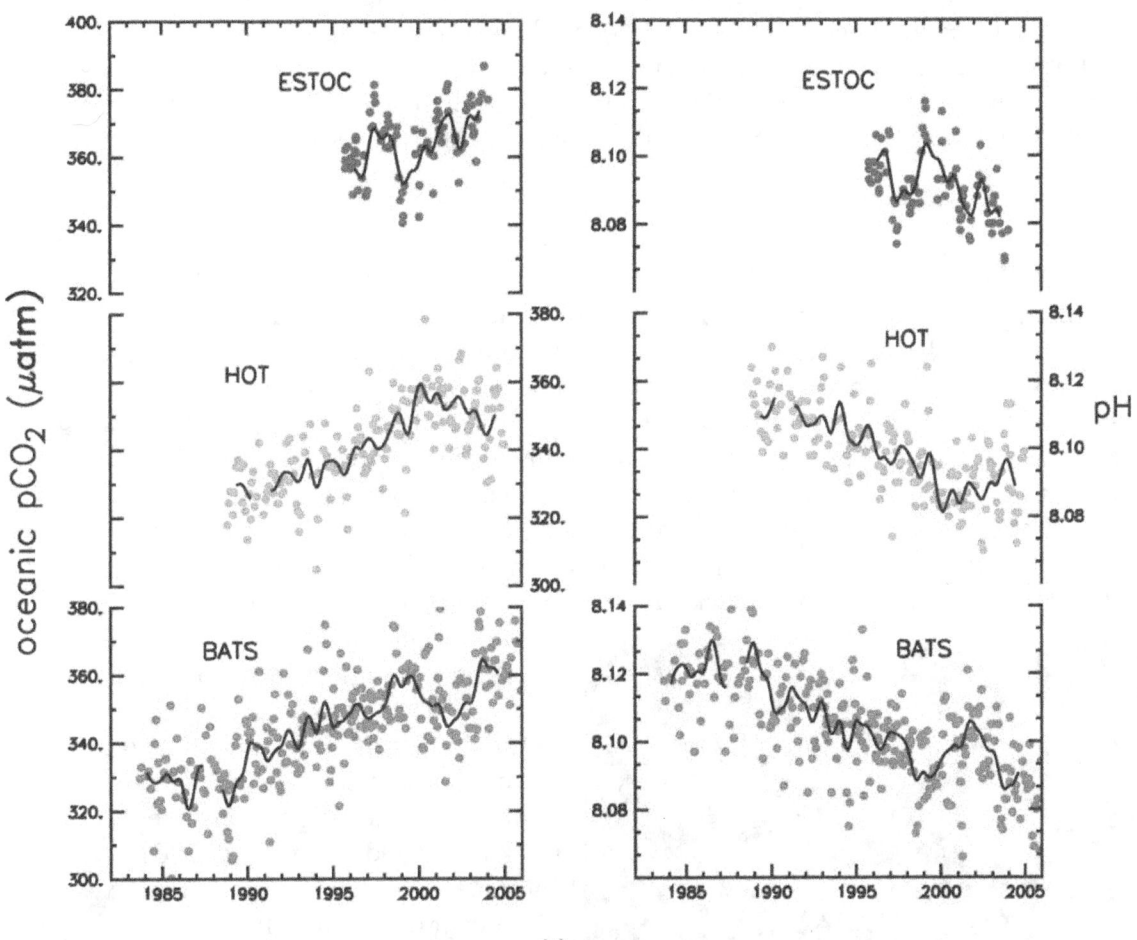

Figure 2.13. Changes in surface oceanic $pCO_2$ (left; in µatm) and pH (right) from three time series stations: Blue: European Station for Time-series in the Ocean (ESTOC, 29°N, 15°W; Gonzalez-Dávila et al. 2003); green: Hawaii Ocean Time-Series (HOT, 23°N, 158°W; Dore et al., 2003); red: Bermuda Atlantic Time-series Study (BATS, 31/32°N, 64°W; Bates et al., 2002; Gruber et al., 2002). Values of $pCO_2$ and pH were calculated from DIC and alkalinity at HOT and BATS; pH was directly measured at ESTOC and $pCO_2$ was calculated from pH and alkalinity. The mean seasonal cycle was removed from all data. The thick black line is smoothed and does not contain variability less than 0.5 years period. Credit: Solomon et al. 2007.

# 3.    Biological Responses to Climate Change

Global climate change will alter the physical environment that sets the stage for biological organisms to perish or flourish. In this way, climate change can be expected to produce "winners" and "losers" (Somero 2010). In coral reef habitats, "losers" may be those species that are unable to compensate for ocean acidification whereas "winners" may be species that benefit from climate change directly (e.g. seagrasses) or those that benefit indirectly through a reduction in competitors (e.g. macroalgae). Climate change can impact organisms in a variety of ways. Climate change may alter the timing of weather events and seasonality with potentially serious impacts on marine species, particularly during sensitive times such as migration, breeding, and early larval stages. It may alter the "optimal" environmental window for a species that could respond by shifting its range to match ideal conditions. The impacts of climate change may also alter the environment for invasive species, potentially increasing their impacts if they are favored under the new conditions. This chapter explores biological mechanisms and specific taxa that may be altered by climate change in FBNMS and throughout American Samoa.

## 3.1.  Ecological Responses

### 3.1.1.  Species Shifts

A potential consequence of climate change is a shift in species' distributions to remain in favorable environments. Theory suggests that in response to warming, species should migrate towards the poles in order to remain in their optimal temperature window (Parmesan 1996). However, species may not only shift their distribution by latitude, they may respond by moving to shallower or deeper waters. For example, with increasing ocean temperatures, coral may begin settling in deeper or more offshore locations in order to find a thermally suitable habitat. Coral has also been observed to settle in locations further from the equator than in recent history. In Florida, species of *Acropora* are now living further north than previously recorded  (Precht and Aronson 2004) (Fig. 3.1).  Areas with increased water flow may also be favored by corals as ocean temperatures increase. This can occur because higher flow rates may confer resistance to bleaching by removing harmful toxins within coral colonies associated with high water temperatures and high irradiance (Nakamura and van Woesik 2001). Intertidal or coastal species shifts may also occur as a result of sea level rise, but shifts in coral communities would also lead to shifts in associated species (e.g., fishes that use coral as refuge). At this time there is insufficient data available to determine whether species shifts have already occurred or are likely to occur at the sanctuary site.

**Figure 3.1. Elkhorn coral, *Acropora palmata* may be expanding their range to the north. Photo Credit: Paige Gill.**

### 3.1.2. Non-native Species

Climate change may allow non-native species to exploit environmental conditions that are novel to an area (Dukes and Mooney 1999). For example, non-native species that require slightly warmer water than currently exists would be able to survive and potentially prosper in elevated ocean temperatures. These species may have been introduced in the past, but were previously unable to survive. If introduced again in future warmer conditions, they may be able to exploit the newly suitable habitat. Also, species that have been introduced and survived in very low numbers due to marginal environmental conditions may experience population growth and compete with native species when the habitat becomes more suitable. Examples include warm-water phytoplankton, macroalgae and fish species that have recently appeared in the Mediterranean and the North Sea (Chisholm et al. 1995, Nehring 1996, Nieder et al. 2000).

Climatically driven changes may affect both local dispersal mechanisms due to the alteration of current patterns, and competitive interactions between non-native and native species due to the onset of new thermal optima and/or different carbonate chemistry (Occhipinti-Ambrogi 2007). For example, an increase in temperature may favor the development of non-native species' larvae, allowing them to out-compete the native species (Stachowicz et al. 2002). In addition to latitudinal range expansions of species and effects on species richness and native species, some invasions may provoke multiple effects that alter overall ecosystem functioning (e.g., material flow between trophic groups, primary production, relative extent of organic material decomposition, extent of benthic-pelagic coupling) (Occhipinti-Ambrogi, 2007).

Evaluating the effects of climate change on non-native species begins by assessing the current status of invasion within the sanctuary. Coles et al. (2003) identified a total of 28 non-native or cryptogenic (i.e., of uncertain origin) species during studies conducted throughout Tutuila in 2002, fewer than the 98 that were observed on harbor surveys in Hawai'i (Coles et al. 1997; 1999a; 1999b). Of these, the cryptogenic species found in Fagatele Bay consisted of the seaweeds *Caulerpa serrulata* and *Halymenia durvillei* as well as the hydroid *Plumularia strictocarpa*. The introduced species consisted of the polychaete *Salmacina dysteri* and the bryozoan *Savignyella lafontii*. At the time of the study, none of the species appeared to be propagating to a degree where they are in competition with native species or spreading beyond a limited distribution concentrated in the dock areas of inner Pago Pago Harbor (Coles et al. 2003). Furthermore, there was no indication that the presence of non-native species occurred as a result of climate change. However there is a need for additional research in this area.

### 3.1.3. Disease Outbreak

The incidence of marine diseases has been projected to increase (Harvell et al. 2002). In particular, the frequency of disease outbreak is likely to increase in species that experience stress due to increasing ocean temperatures. Evidence from the Caribbean also suggests that diseases on coral reefs have already become more numerous (Goreau et al. 1998). Increased stress levels results in immunosuppression in organisms, thus increasing their vulnerability to infections. This is observed in tropical corals, which live at the edge of their thermal maxima and are more susceptible to disease infections after bleaching (Rosenberg and Ben-Haim 2002, Brandt and McManus 2009). Also of concern is an increase in the populations of existing potentially harmful bacteria due to increased ocean temperatures. Novel bacteria, which may have previously been unable to tolerate the temperature or pH range, may be able to exploit the new conditions brought by climate change.

One specific disease of concern to the sanctuary is "coralline lethal orange disease" (CLOD). CLOD is a disease of bacterial origin that has affected coralline algae throughout the south Pacific (Littler and Littler 1995; Aeby 2007) (Fig. 3.2). In the sanctuary site, CLOD was found to be common from shallow water down to 12 m (40 ft) depth transects (Birkeland et al. 2003). Diseases affecting coralline algae are significant because corallines are important to reef health. Corallines stabilize the reef by growing over and cementing dead corals. Also, larvae of many

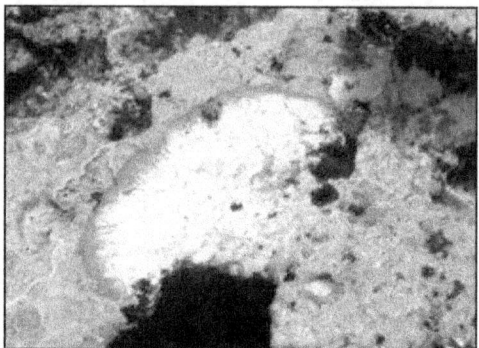

**Figure 3.2.Coralline lethal orange disease in Fagatele Bay National Marine Sanctuary. Photo Credit: Bill Kiene.**

reef-building corals respond to chemical cues from coralline algae as signals or stimulants for settling and/or undergoing metamorphosis (Birkeland et al. 2003). Coralline algae also exhibit an encrusting growth form, preventing fleshy or filamentous algal growth and provide smooth clean substrata on which corals can settle. In contrast, filamentous and fleshy algae abrade and overgrow coral recruits, while also producing sediment traps that smother small corals (Birkeland et al. 2003). While it is unknown if climate change may directly affect the occurrence of CLOD at the sanctuary site, conditions that create additional stress for coralline algae may predispose it to increased incidence of disease.

### 3.1.4. Phenology

Phenology refers to the study of repeated life cycle events and their timing. Examples of these life cycle events include migration, reproduction and the transition from one developmental stage to another. Climate change can negatively affect marine organisms by altering the timing of these events so that they become "mismatched" with other key events ("match mis-match hypothesis" *sensu* Cushing 1990). This can occur if one species is relatively fixed in its development (e.g. fish development) and its prey is highly influenced by climate conditions (e.g. copepods that serve as prey for fish).

Shifts in the timing of phytoplankton blooms demonstrate that the level of response differs throughout the community and seasonal cycle, leading to a mismatch between trophic levels and functional groups (Edwards and Richardson 2004). Many organisms dependent on temperature to stimulate physiological developments and larval release have significantly moved forward in their seasonal cycle in response to warming over the last decade (Edwards and Richardson 2004).

Spawning in marine species is often times photo-period or lunar synchronized, with temperature or tides being a secondary cue. In Palau, coral spawning appears to coincide with the rise toward and fall from the peak amount of solar energy that falls upon an area (i.e. solar insolation maxima) (Penland et al. 2003). Two insolation maxima (a consequence of the vernal and autumnal equinoxes) in Palau lead to multiple spawning events per year. In American Samoa, it appears that coral spawn once per year around the time of the palolo rising, which is in late

October to early November (D. Fenner, *personal communication*). Neither of these primary cues is expected to change with climate change; however, temperature as a secondary cue may result in a drift from the usual time of spawning.

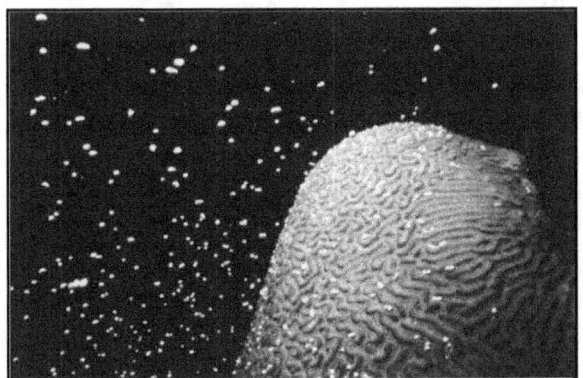

**Figure 3.3.Brain coral spawning, Photo: Emma Hickerson.**

Other marine species in or near the sanctuary may be impacted by the effects of climate change on phenology. In addition to the serious ecological disruption these alterations may cause (e.g., a decoupling of predator/prey cycles); many of these species are also commercially and culturally important. Other species that rely on temperature as a cue for life cycle events may alter the timing of their migrations or breeding, such as birds and whales. Many birds make long distance migrations, such as the local golden plover (*Pluvialis dominica*), wandering tattler (*Heteroscelus incanus*), and ruddy turnstone (*Arenaria interpres*) who migrate from American Samoa to Alaska every year (A.Tagarino, *personal communication*).

### 3.1.5. Calcification

The reduction in available carbonate ions presents a serious problem for skeleton and shell building organisms, which use carbonate ions for the formation of calcium carbonate (Orr et al. 2005; Fabry et al. 2008; Doney et al. 2009). In the tropics, scleractinian corals and calcareous green and red algae are important to the building and cementation of the massive carbonate framework that forms the habitat for coral reef organisms. These taxa produce aragonite and high magnesium calcium skeletons, which are more soluble forms of calcium carbonate. Once conditions are severe enough that tropical waters are significantly impacted by acidification, corals and calcareous algae may be among the first organisms to be impaired. The average response of corals to a doubling of $pCO_2$ is a 30 percent decline in calcification (Kleypas et al. 2006).

In the region American Samoa is located; calcification rates are projected to decrease with climate change over time, but not as rapidly as higher latitudes (Kleypas et al. 1999). Calcification rates in American Samoa may have already decreased approximately 10% from rates prior to the Industrial Revolution (1880). Rates may decrease an additional 10-20% by the year 2100, based on model projections (Kleypas et al. 1999).

While increased $CO_2$ has clearly been shown to reduce calcification rates, there are interactive effects of saturation state, temperature, light, and nutrients that also contribute to the calcification rates of reef organisms. Saturation state is defined here as the degree to which seawater is saturated with respect to carbonate minerals (typically given as $\Omega$). In addition, human activities are causing changes in all of these factors (Kleypas et al. 2006). If seawater chemistry was the only variable affecting calcification, then calcification records from corals and other organisms should show a decrease in calcification over the past century, however this is not always the case (Lough and Barnes 1997; 2000). This is believed to reflect the effects of other variables on calcification, temperature in particular (Lough and Barnes, 1997; 2000, Bessat and Buigues 2001; Carricart-Ganivet 2004). In a study using isotopic analysis of a massive *Porites* coral core from Flinders Reef in the southwest Pacific, there appeared to be a pH flux in the region between about 7.9 and 8.2 units over the last 300 years, in 50-year cycles consistent with circulation changes associated with the Interdecadal Pacific Oscillation (Pelejero et al. 2005). The authors found that calcification rates for this core were not correlated with pH or saturation state, suggesting that the coral sampled is well adapted to large fluctuations in environmental conditions.

How decreased calcification rates will affect the long-term survival of benthic calcifiers is unknown. The effects of reduced calcification on an organism's fitness and survivorship have been hypothesized based on the putative functions of $CaCO_3$ in that organism. In corals and coralline algae, skeletal growth is thought to elevate the organism above the substrate and into higher light and better flow conditions, provide anchoring/rigidity against hydrodynamic forces, increase competitiveness for space, increase light gathering, and provide protection. Furthermore, the reproductive success of some coral species could be affected by slower or more fragile growth. For example, reproductive maturity in *Goniastrea aspera* is achieved by size rather than age (Sakai 1998a; 1998b). Also increased skeletal fragmentation in *Acropora palmata* can promote asexual propagation, but can also lower the potential for sexual reproduction of the species (Lirman 2000). Long- term studies examining the performance of calcifiers and other marine organisms are lacking.

The role of calcification in multiple life stages may play a critical role in organismal survival. For many organisms, the function of $CaCO_3$ varies with life cycle, but almost all studies of $CO_2$ effects on calcification have focused on adults. Agegian (1985) noted that recruitment of coralline algae on aquarium walls was reduced in experiments with elevated $pCO_2$, and Green et al. (2004) found that newly settled larvae of the mollusc *Mercenaria mercenaria* experienced higher shell dissolution and mortality rates when the pore-water interface was under saturated with respect to aragonite. Studies that evaluate the effect of ocean acidification on multiple life stages of marine organisms are clearly needed.

While acidification studies are still in their infancy, they are becoming more common and tractable with increasing awareness and technological capability. In the last NOAA Coral Reef Ecosystem Division (CRED) cruise to American Samoa, several autonomous pH meters were deployed which will reveal time series pH data over the next two years. In addition, there is a project proposed for the airport pools, which will test the feasibility of increasing pH *in situ*. Increased data and plans for further research on mitigating acidification impacts on coral reefs will put American Samoa in a better position to deal with the challenges of climate change.

## 3.2. Taxonomic Response

### 3.2.1. Corals

There are over 200 identified species of coral in the reefs of the sanctuary. Corals serve an important role in coral reef ecosystems because they provide shelter and habitat for the abundant varieties of marine life that make coral reefs their home. Ocean warming, ocean acidification, and changes to tropical cyclone intensity are the primary climate change drivers of concern for this taxonomic group.

### 3.2.1.1. Coral Larval Development

Elevated ocean temperatures have the potential to negatively affect the development and survivorship of reef coral larvae. Tropical hermatypic corals tend to live close to their thermal maxima during summer months (Coles and Brown 2003; Jokiel 2004), thus the additional increase in ocean temperatures due to climate change can have detrimental effects (Glynn 1993; Williams and Bunkley-Williams 1990; Brown 1997; Hoegh-Guldberg 1999).

A major Caribbean reef-building coral, *Acropora palmata*, reproduces annually during August and September (periods of elevated ocean temperature). Randall and Szmant (2009) investigated the effects of elevated temperatures on development, survival, and larval settlement of *A. palmata* by culturing newly fertilized eggs at temperatures ranging from 27.5-31.5 °C, which are within the temperature range for near shore reefs in American Samoa (K. Anderson, *unpublished data*).

They found that development was accelerated and the percentage of developmental abnormalities increased at higher temperatures. Larvae cultured at 30 and 31.5 °C experienced as much as an 8-fold decrease in survivorship compared to those at 28 °C. Settlement was found to be 62% at 28 °C compared to 37% at 31.5 °C. These results indicate that embryos and larvae of *A. palmata* will be negatively affected as sea surface temperatures continue to warm. These results may be similar in other coral species, particularly those that spawn during periods of elevated ocean temperature. However, additional studies are needed to determine if warming and acidification will result in negative impacts on coral larvae as a general phenomenon.

**Figure 3.4. Over 200 species of coral have been identified in the sanctuary. Photo Credit: FBNMS.**

### 3.2.1.2. Coral Bleaching

Coral bleaching, a phenomenon named after the white color of the coral skeletons that are visible once bleached, is a loss of the coral's endosymbiont, zooxanthellae. Zooxanthellae are a type of single-celled dinoflagellate algae of the genus *Symbiodinium*, which live in the shared tissues of coral and are able to move about within the colony. Coral and zooxanthellae have a symbiotic relationship whereby the coral can receive up to 90 percent of their daily energy needs from zooxanthellae (Marshall and Schuttenberg 2006). In return, the zooxanthellae receive shelter. When conditions become stressful to the coral, they are thought to eject or consume the zooxanthellae. Elevated temperature and light levels may also result in the production of reactive oxygen species by the zooxanthellae, which can damage coral cellular structures (Marshall and Schuttenberg 2006).

Bleaching frequency and intensity will increase with increasing sea temperatures unless corals are capable of adapting to greater temperatures. Coral bleaching is a major concern with ramifications reaching far after the event ends. If corals are able to regain their zooxanthellae in time, they will not die. However, the stress of bleaching severely depletes their energy reserves; leaving some species more vulnerable to infection as well as leaving less energy for growth and reproduction. Many species of coral that have bleached will typically not spawn that year (Hoegh-Guldberg 1999; Ward et al. 2000, Fenner et al. 2008), meaning coral that annually bleaches will be relegated to asexual reproduction, thus reducing the genetic diversity of the colonies and potentially their evolutionary fitness.

**Figure 3.5.Coral bleaching, Fagatele Bay National Marine Sanctuary. Photo Credit: Charles Birkeland.**

Other research on the ramifications of coral bleaching on reproduction includes Fine and Loya (2003), who demonstrated that bleaching reduces the energy available for competition with other benthic organisms. Szmant and Gassman (1990) described a failure in gametogenesis by *Montrastraea annularis* following bleaching. Ward et al. (2000) reported a reduction in the number of eggs and percent of fertile polyps in a variety of bleached species on the Great Barrier Reef. Bleaching reduced both egg size and number in the soft coral, *Lobophytum compactum* (Michalek-Wagner and Willis 2001). Omori et al. (2001) demonstrated reduced fertilization rates for bleached corals in Okinawa, and Mendes and Woodley (2002) found a reduced number of gonads per polyp in *M. annuularis* following bleaching.

Promisingly, American Samoa does have some unique pool environments where corals withstand large fluctuations in temperature, light, pH, and dissolved oxygen (Craig et al. 2001; Smith 2008). On Tutuila Island, the "airport pools" in the village of Tafuna and on Ofu Island to the east, back reef pools with high coral abundance deal with daily pH swings of 0.1 in addition to temperature ranges of 6°C (up to 32°C ) and reduced dissolved oxygen (P. Craig, *personal communication*). Several studies have asked why these corals appear well adapted to this wide range of variables (Craig et al. 2001; Smith and Birkeland 2003; Smith 2008). However, it appears that the cause for this adaptation is still unknown. It may be an example of place-based evolution (i.e., those corals having evolved in place are adapted to it). Interestingly, there is very little bleaching in the Ofu pools (Smith 2008) while the pools at Pago Pago International airport show annual bleaching (Fenner et al. 2008; Fenner and Heron 2009). Annual bleaching in the airport pools is usually limited to the upper portion of the horizontal branches of *Acropora* corals; since staghorns are not as abundant in the Ofu pools, it is possible this could partially explain the discrepancy in bleaching patterns. The resiliency of corals in these back reef pools of Ofu suggests that corals may have the capacity to cope with brief elevated temperatures. Those species adapted to environments with steep $CO_2$ gradients, such as hydrothermal vents or stagnant tide pools, and those species with high capacity for metabolic production of $CO_2$ may have evolved greater capacities for buffering, ion exchange, and $CO_2$ transport (Seibel and Walsh 2001; 2003). Whether such elevated capacity translates into greater tolerance of chronic ocean acidification remains unknown.

### 3.2.1.3. Responses to Sea Level Anomalies

In American Samoa, negative sea surface height anomalies have resulted in the exposure of corals and fatal conditions for large areas of reef flats. In order for coral to be exposed to air, a low tide must coincide with a large negative sea surface height anomaly, such as from an ENSO event. The risk of exposure to air is serious and results in mortality in most cases (Pirhalla et al. 2010).

The interannual changes in mean sea level of up to -30 cm may not appear to be of a significant magnitude to impact to coral reef ecosystems (Figure 3). Anomalies of this magnitude are not uncommon in the Pacific where the major positive shifts in mean sea level occur in response to sub-regional warm (and consequently low density) patches of ocean, which may persist for several months (Mitchell et al. 2001). However, because of the long periodicity of these extreme anomalies, there is sufficient time for coral to grow to the limit of mean lower low sea level. Thus, when these prolonged extreme low tides occur, they can seriously impact the coral within the top 30 cm of the water column. Much of the Samoan shoreline is composed of reef flats, and in older coral colonies it is easy to see evidence of coral that has been "topped" (flattened on its upper surface due to exposure at lower low tide). Coral colonies and branches within the same colony are observed to achieve a remarkably uniform upper limit to vertical growth, within 1-2 cm (Pirhalla et al. 2010). It should be noted that these changes in sea surface height, as much as 30 cm, is far larger than annual changes in sea level due to climate change, which are on the order of 2-3 mm.

Increased mean sea level will not have such immediate and pernicious impacts to coral as exposure to air can cause, however in the future there may be serious consequences. Most species of coral are able to keep up with the predicted sea level rise rate, provided they are healthy (Smith and Buddemeier 1992). For those capable of growing at a rate comparable to the rate of sea level rise, their ability to continue this growth rate may be reduced due to the increasingly difficult conditions they will face with higher temperatures and reduced pH. The additional thermal stress and ocean acidification reduce energy available for growth, thus potentially rendering coral unable to keep up with sea level rise. Most likely, mass bleaching events will simply kill the corals on the reef flat. However, coralline algae on the reef flat will survive bleaching events and continue to grow (D. Fenner, *personal communication*).

### 3.2.1.4. Habitat Change

With coral comprising the primary habitat structure, there is a high potential for a change in habitat from climate change impacts such as increased ocean temperatures and $CO_2$ levels. After bleaching, corals are more susceptible to diseases in their weakened state (Fenner et al. 2008 and references therein), and if the coral does not regain its zooxanthellae it will die. Dead coral skeletons can be recolonized given the right conditions; however, prolonged periods of elevated water temperatures will prevent this from occurring quickly. If the skeletons are not recolonized within a few weeks, they will be overgrown with algae. If these algae are coralline algae, this is not a total loss as the coral larvae will settle on coralline algae. However if the skeleton is overgrown with fleshy algae it becomes unsuitable for recolonization by coral. In the latter case, the skeleton will eventually be eroded and turned into rubble which can further damage surrounding colonies by abrading them during high wave or current action.

The collapse of coral skeletons will also result in a loss of rugosity (a measure of habitat complexity). More complex habitat structure allows more area for fish and invertebrates to shelter and feed in. If coral skeletons on the outer reef slope collapse, this may also result in wave action continuing further onto shore unimpeded. This energy will begin eroding previously protected coral, which is unaccustomed to this level of wave energy.

The potential loss of coral cover is a serious concern for the terrestrial habitats as well. Coral reefs act as break waters for waves, reducing coastal erosion by absorbing wave energy. This is particularly important in typhoons or tsunamis. An example can be seen at Rose Atoll, the U.S. national marine monument that lies 170 miles (270km) to the east of Tutuila in American Samoa. At Rose, where the lagoon arms are composed primarily of calcified coralline algae, a reduction in calcification rates may lead to reduced integrity of the protective lagoon arms and potentially a reduction in their height. This would allow more over-wash of waves, which may lead to increased erosion of Rose and Sand Islands.

### 3.2.1.5. Siltation

Average siltation may decrease with decreased rainfall, although the buildup of loose sediment due to lack of rain could result in large inputs of sediment when rain does occur. Sediment is extremely detrimental to coral in general, causing an increased expenditure of energy and reducing fecundity, and specifically to the resilience of coral in Fagatele Bay and the rest of American Samoa (*sensu* Birkeland et al. 1987). According to a 2006-2007 survey by the Department of Marine and Wildlife Resources, the average sedimentation rate is 12.1 $g/cm^2/day$ in bays, compared to 1.4 $g/cm^2/day$ at topographic high points (i.e. highest elevation) (Fenner et al. 2008).The sedimentation rate from stream sites was much higher than bay or point sites at 84.7 $g/cm^2/day$ (Fenner et al. 2008). High rates of sedimentation such as those found at stream mouths were considered detrimental to coral reefs while rates at the bays and points were considered to have moderate and slight effects, respectively (Pastorok and Bilyard 1985).

### 3.2.2. Invertebrates

The total number of invertebrates currently inhabiting Fagatele Bay is unknown however over 1,400 species of algae and invertebrates have been identified in the coral reefs around Tutuila. Marine invertebrates will respond to a variety of climate change drivers, perhaps most notably of which are ocean warming, ocean acidification, changing nutrient concentrations and subsequent primary production as well as increased intensity of tropical cyclones.

Warming will have impacts on marine invertebrates because nearly all regulate body temperatures through external means (i.e. they are ectothermic). Indeed, temperature effects on marine organisms are found across all levels of biological organization. Warming may result in the production of heat shock proteins and effects on other molecular processes, potentially impaired organ function, or mortality if severe enough (Somero 2010). Contrary to expectation, warm adapted species (such as those in the

**Figure 3.6.** *Vasidae vasum* in **American Samoa. Photo Credit: NOAA CRED.**

tropics) may be particularly susceptible to greater temperatures because they possess reduced ability to deal with thermal challenges (Stillman 2003). Warming is also known to consistently modify the length of time that larvae spend in the water column (O'Connor et al. 2007). Therefore, warming in addition to changes in ocean circulation will likely influence the transport of larvae. This is particularly important for benthic invertebrates associated with islands. Here, the potential for larvae to be "lost at sea" is greater and processes that influence larval transport can have even greater effects on population persistence or recovery.

Several studies have demonstrated physiological stress in invertebrates exposed to very high $pCO_2$ levels that would be expected from direct $CO_2$ disposal in the ocean (Brewer et al. 2004, see also review in Doney et al. 2009). The physiological and calcification effects of long-term exposure of mollusks and sea urchins to ocean acidification were recently investigated by two studies. Specimens of the mussel, *Mytilus galloprovincialis*, were maintained for three months at pH = 7.3 (consistent with a $pCO_2$ of 1900 µatm) and experienced a significant reduction in growth, as well as shell dissolution, in response to reduced haemolymph bicarbonate levels (Michaelidis et al. 2005). In another study, specimens of two species of sea urchin (*Hemicentrotus pulcherrimus* and *Echinometra mathaei*) and one gastropod mollusc (*Strombus luhuanus*) that were exposed for six months to $CO_2$ levels elevated by 200 ppm over normal levels had smaller size and body weight, and in *E. mathaei* a thinning of the $CaCO_3$ skeleton was observed (Shirayama and Thornton 2005). Many other calcifying taxa are important ecologically, economically, culturally, and as components of the marine $CaCO_3$ cycle (e.g., calcareous green algae, echinoderms, benthic mollusks and foraminifera, bryozoans, ahermatypic corals).

### 3.2.3. Phytoplankton and Macroalgae

Phytoplankton may respond to changes to a variety of environmental conditions that are linked to climate change. These include increased temperature, enhanced surface stratification, intensification or weakening of nutrient upwelling, stimulation of photosynthesis by elevated $CO_2$, changes in land runoff and nutrient availability, and altered ocean pH. Phytoplankton need to remain close to the ocean's surface in order to capture sunlight for photosynthesis. If surface waters become depleted of nutrients required for growth, overall phytoplankton biomass may decline. Indeed, the area of low primary productivity in the tropical oceans has been increasing (Polovina et al. 2008). The increase in oligotrophic waters is in part attributed to increased temperature and may be linked to water column stratification. Decreased nutrient availability may also favor phytoplankton differently. For example, dinoflagellates are distinguished by the presence of two flagella used for swimming. Other phytoplankton groups, such as diatoms, do not possess this swimming ability, and therefore do not have the potential to undergo vertical migration for nutrients deeper in the water

**Figure 3.7. Caulerpa phytoplankton in American Samoa. Photo Credit: NOAA CRED.**

column. Nutrients in the surface layer of the water column can become limited through a combination of phytoplankton uptake and the decrease in upward mixing of nutrients under a stratified water column. The swimming ability of dinoflagellates allows them to swim below the upper stratified layer of the water column to utilize nutrients in the deeper layer that other phytoplankton cannot access (Falkowski et al. 2004). Dinoflagellates are therefore expected to be favored over other phytoplankton in marine environments under future climate scenarios.

It is possible that the frequency of marine dinoflagellate harmful algal blooms may increase as a result of climate change (Hallegraeff 1993, Vitousek 1997). While harmful algal blooms are not known to occur around American Samoa, there have been non-toxic red tides in Pago Pago harbor that have turned the entire harbor red. Warmer temperatures may result in expanded ranges of warm water dinoflagellate species. For example, the tropical marine dinoflagellate, *Gambierdiscus toxicus,* has been documented in Samoa and is associated with ciguatera fish poisoning. It primarily occurs as an epiphyte on some macroalgae (Rey 2007). The abundance of *G. toxicus* correlates positively with elevated sea surface temperature during the warm phases of the ENSO cycle (Hales et al. 1999, Chateau-Degat et al. 2005) and its range may extend to higher latitudes as temperatures rise (Tester 1994). Indirect effects of climate change may also locally increase habitat for *G. toxicus* to proliferate. Perturbations to coral reefs, such as hurricanes or bleaching events caused by increased water temperatures, may free up space for host macroalgae to colonize. Greater available habitat (i.e. macroalgae) could therefore increase ciguatera incidents.

Increased $CO_2$ may increase the rate of macroalgal growth, and specifically that of fleshy algae rather than coralline algae. Coralline algae are slower growing than fleshy algae under "normal" $CO_2$ conditions and significant increases in dissolved $CO_2$ inhibits formation of their calcite carbonate skeleton (Kuffner et al. 2008, Martin and Gattuso 2009). The incidence of CLOD may also reduce the abundance of coralline algae; potentially creating favorable conditions for macroalgal growth, though so far it is far outstripped by the ability of the coralline algae to grow, especially in Fagatele Bay.

Changes in seawater $CO_2$ concentrations and ocean acidification are also likely to influence phytoplankton species assemblages. These additional inorganic carbon sources, from bicarbonate and $CO_2$ can be utilized by primary producers for photosynthesis and growth. Seagrasses are an example of a marine plant that also directly uses $CO_2$ for photosynthesis and which may benefit from increased $CO_2$ concentrations (Zimmerman et al. 1997; Invers et al. 2001; Invers et al. 2002; Palacios and Zimmerman 2007).

In summary, climate change could be expected to impact phytoplankton and macroalgae in the following ways: (i) range expansion of warm-water species at the expense of coldwater species which are driven polewards, (ii) changes in the abundance and seasonal window of growth of selected harmful algal bloom species, (iii) earlier timing of peak production of some phytoplankton, (iv) cascading effects for marine food webs, notably when individual zooplankton and fish grazers are differentially impacted by climate change. Some harmful algal bloom phenomena (e.g., toxic dinoflagellates benefiting from land runoff and/or water column stratification, tropical benthic dinoflagellates responding to coral reef disturbance) may become worse, while others may diminish in areas currently impacted.

### 3.2.4.  Fish

Coral reefs of Fagatele Bay provide habitat for at least 271 species of fish. Abundant groups include adult and juvenile damselfish, surgeonfish, wrasse, butterfly fish, and small parrotfish. Potential climate change impacts include elevated temperatures, reduced pH, and altered dissolved oxygen levels. These impacts can cause serious complications for fish at multiple life stages. Ocean acidification studies have found deleterious impacts of acidification on fish and their larvae (see 2.4: "Ocean Acidification" chapter). Recruitment in fish populations has long been known to be a key process that is strongly influenced by climate variability (Cushing 1995). Variations in atmospheric circulation over the Bering Sea, through interactions with ocean currents, influence transportation of juvenile walleye pollock (*Theragra chalcogramma*) away from adults, affecting the intensity of cannibalism and, consequently, year class strength (Wespestad et al. 2000).

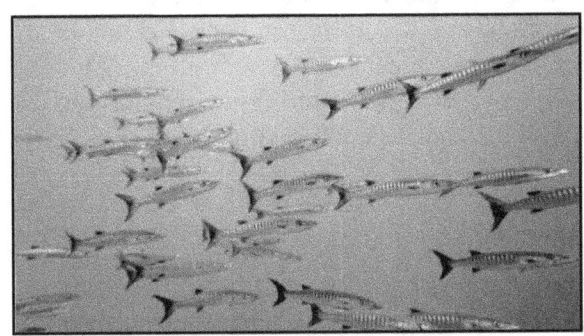

**Figure 3.8.Baracuda in American Samoa. Photo Credit: Kerry Grimshaw, NOAA CRED.**

Mora and Ospína (2001) examined the physiological thermal tolerance of 15 fishes from the tropical eastern Pacific Ocean. They found that the tolerance ranged from 34.7 to 40.8 °C, greater than temperatures recorded in most areas around American Samoa, however a few pool environments have occasionally reached 35 °C (P. Craig, *personal communication*). Other factors impacting the survival of fish (e.g., magnitude and duration of high temperature exposure) are also important for predicting fish's response and survival, and peak temperatures in pools of 35 °C occur for only very brief periods. Sufficient temperature increases may affect immune system function, and decrease fecundity in coral reef fishes (Bevelhimer and Bennett 2000, Mora and Ospína 2001).

Population persistence of most coastal marine species depends on larvae finding suitable adult habitat at the end of a dispersive stage, which can last weeks or months. This is particularly important for island species that may experience high larval mortality if larvae are swept out to the open ocean where there is no suitable habitat. Populations of the same species on different or the same island may therefore be "connected" by this dispersal stage (referred to as "population connectivity"). The degree of population connectivity is influenced by physical factors such as ocean currents, as well as biological factors such as the amount of time spent in the plankton or larval behavior. Climate change can alter the degree of population connectivity by modifying ocean currents or temperature, which affects the amount of time spent in the water column (see Kendall and Poti for in depth discussion, Munday et al. 2008). Other climate change effects such as ocean acidification may affect the ability of larvae to detect olfactory cues to locate appropriate adult habitat (Munday et al. 2009). Larval clownfish (*Amphiprion percula*) reared in control seawater (pH 8.15) were able to discriminate between a range of cues that could help them locate suitable settlement sites. This discriminatory ability was disrupted when larvae were reared in conditions simulating ocean acidification. Larvae became strongly attracted to olfactory stimuli they normally avoided when reared at levels of ocean pH that could occur *ca.* 2100 (pH 7.8) and they no longer responded to any olfactory cues when reared at pH levels (pH 7.6) that might be attained later next century on a business-as-usual carbon-dioxide emissions trajectory (pH 7.6). If acidification continues unabated, the impairment of sensory ability could inhibit the ability of organisms to locate settlement sites in addition to other sensory dependent functions (e.g. foraging or mating).

Ocean acidification has also been documented to affect other physiological processes in marine fish. Impacts range from increased ventilation (Reviewed in Truchot 1987, Hayashi et al. 2004), reduced cardiac output (Ishimatsu et al. 2004), reduced metabolic capacity (Michaelidis et al. 2007), reduced feed intake (Cecchini et al. 2001), and death (Kikkawa et al. 2003; Hayashi et al. 2004, Ishimatsu et al. 2005; Kikkawa et al. 2006). While these impacts are severe, the conditions under which the fish were tested were more extreme than projections indicate our oceans will become. Mortality occurred in three fish species tested, including yellowtail and flounder, only at very high $CO_2$ levels (>50,000 ppmv) after 24 h exposure, and the authors concluded that fish mortality caused by anthropogenic $CO_2$ is never expected in marine environments (Hayashi et al. 2004). While that statement may be premature, marine fish do appear highly tolerant of $CO_2$ (Kikkawa et al. 2004; 2006). The hatchling stages of some species appeared fairly sensitive to pH decreases on the order of 0.5 or greater, but high $CO_2$ tolerance developed within a few days of hatching (Ishimatsu et al. 2004).

### 3.2.5. Whales

The migratory paths of humpback whales in the southern hemisphere intersect with American Samoa. Each year, from July through October, humpbacks use the waters around American Samoa for breeding and calving. Occasionally sperm whales venture into the water surrounding American Samoa and may be seen seaward of Fagatele Bay. Potential climate impacts to whales may occur in polar areas as ice retreats, but due to the migratory nature of these animals, these

**Figure 3.9. Humpback Whale in American Samoa. Photo Credit: David Mattilla, NOAA, ONMS.**

effects may be seen in whales that migrate to American Samoa. Potential impacts include alterations in habitat availability, which may be influenced by factors such as ocean currents and water temperature; food availability, as changes may lead to decreased productivity and altered patterns of prey distribution and availability; and increasing diseases, as climatic changes could introduce exposure to novel or resurging diseases. Currently most of the concern about emerging or resurging cetacean diseases associated with climate change has focused on their feeding grounds, as some scientists around the world have noticed increases in diseases in those habitats that may be associated with climate change (IWC 2007).

Humpbacks do not generally forage during their time in American Samoa waters because it is a breeding ground, although opportunistic feeding may occur on their way to breeding grounds (A. Tagarino, *personal communication*). If there were any increase in sexually transmitted diseases, they would likely occur in American Samoa (D. Matilla, *personal communication*). There is also evidence that some baleen whales may migrate further poleward in order to find the food resources they require (D. Matilla, *personal communication*). This may result in prolonged migrations, with subsequent energy and timing consequences, or a shift in breeding grounds to reduce the distance traveled (Simmonds et al. 2009). Ocean acidification may also affect the absorption of sound in seawater (Hester et al. 2008). Given a decrease in pH of 0.3, sound absorption decreases by 40%, potentially increasing the effect of manmade noise on marine mammals as well as all other auditory communication in the ocean.

### 3.2.6. Sea Turtles

Hawksbill (*Eretmochelys imbricata*) and green sea turtles (*Chelonia mydas*) are frequently seen in Fagatele Bay. At the time that this document was written, no comprehensive studies on the potential impacts of climate change on sea turtles have been conducted in American Samoa. However, studies conducted elsewhere in the world indicate that sea turtles may be vulnerable to potential impacts from climate change. Marine sea turtles have temperature dependent sex determination, having a 1:1 sex ratio at a specific or "pivotal" temperature. Above this temperature the sex ratio shifts in favor of females, and below this temperature the ratio favors males (Jazen and Paukstis 1991; Mrosovsky and Pieau 1991). The nesting season in the Manu'a Islands in American Samoa is generally September to June. Turtle nesting on Tutuila Island is rare and sporadic however data suggests that nesting occurs year round (A. Tagarino, *personal communication*, 2010). Under the projected scenarios of climate change, warmer summers may result in a shift toward female dominated hatchlings. Concern exists that if this trend continues, it could end in extinction for sea turtles (Davenport 1989; 1997; Matsuzawa et al. 2002). On Ascension Island in the South Atlantic Ocean, there has been a measured increase in nest temperature of a green

**Figure 3.10. Green sea turtles are found within the sanctuary but no studies have been conducted on climate change impacts to this species or hawksbill turtles which are also found in the region. Photo: David Burdick, NOAA.**

sea turtle rookery between 0.36°C and 0.49°C for the last 100 years (Hayes et al. 2003). Turtles on this island produce many female hatchlings (up to 99.4%) (Godley et al. 2001), suggesting that beaches with cooler conditions (i.e. sand with higher reflectance) may become increasingly important in the production of male sea turtles (Hayes et al. 2003).

# 4.   Parallel Ecosystem Stressors

In addition to the threats from climate change, there are also several other stressors that may adversely affect the sanctuary site. These stressors may interact with climate change drivers to produce cumulative impacts on biodiversity and ecosystem health (Vinebrooke et al. 2004, Breitburg et al. 1998, Frost et al. 1999, Schindler 2001). Some examples of interacting ecosystem stressors within the sanctuary include fishing, crown-of-thorns starfish outbreak, agriculture, and visitation. Both locally induced stress and climate change stress reduce the resilience of ecosystems – the capacity of systems to keep functioning even when disturbed (Levin and Lubchenco, 2008). Thus, in order to assess the possible impacts of climate change on ecosystems in the sanctuary, the existence of parallel stressors due to local human influences must also be recognized.

## 4.1.  Fishing

Although most fishing methods are prohibited in Fagatele Bay National Marine Sanctuary, the sanctuary's remote location makes enforcement of regulations difficult. There is evidence that fishing may occur in the bay. Several large species of reef fish that are characteristic of unfished reefs in the Indo-Pacific region are conspicuously absent or are small in size in Fagatele Bay. These species include Maori wrasse (humphead wrasse; Napoleon wrasse; *Cheilinus undulates*), parrotfish (bumphead Parrotfish *Bolbometopon muricatum*), sharks, and large species of grouper, all of which are known to be particularly vulnerable to fishing pressure. Given that many of these species are more abundant and larger in size elsewhere in the Pacific where fishing is banned, these observations suggest that historical and current fishing pressure on the reefs of American Samoa and Fagatele Bay has had a significant impact on fish populations.

**Figure 4.1. A Fisherman on Tutuila with a large Maori wrasse. These fish have become extremely rare on American Samoa's reefs.  Photo Credit: Leslie Clift.**

Because of its remote location and limited access from land, direct observation of fishing activity, both legal and illegal, is difficult to obtain. However, it is possible that illegal fishing occurs within the sanctuary when weather conditions permit, and in December 2005, law enforcement officials apprehended illegal fishermen in the sanctuary. Fishermen have the potential to very quickly reduce the population of commercial reef fish species in a small area such as Fagatele Bay. One particularly efficient harvesting technique is spearfishing at night using SCUBA equipment. Many targeted species rest on the reef during the night, making them easy targets. The Government of American Samoa banned SCUBA spearfishing in 2001 because of concerns by local scientists about declines in fish numbers once this technique became widely used.

Evidence also suggests that destructive fishing with

34

explosives has occurred in the bay.

A 2001 survey found a large *Porites* sp. coral colony that was severely damaged. The colony had been split in two, and one side appeared to have been reduced to rubble. It is likely that explosives caused this damage because approximately 9 meters of detonation cord was found adjacent to the coral colony. Although the damage can still be seen, the colony remains healthy away from the fracture. In June 2005, a new round of fishing with explosives was documented in Fagatele Bay. A reward for information yielded no suspects, but did bring attention to the problem and a public desire for the apprehension of anyone fishing in this manner.

Illegal and destructive fishing can stress fishery populations. Overstressed fishery populations are vulnerable to potential impacts from climate change including shifting current patterns (Hughs et al. 2005 in Keller et al. 2008). Overfishing has also been shown to reduce mean life span as well as lifetime reproductive success and larval quality, making fished species more susceptible climate change impacts (Keller et al. 2008). Large keystone species, such as apex predators, have major effects on ecosystems and their loss has potentially great effects on reef resilience. When the population of an apex predator is threatened it can destabilize ecosystems by removing the limiting pressure on their prey and making the ecosystem more susceptible to climate change stressors. Large fish with late maturity are slow to recover, particularly for sharks which generally have 2-4 pups per year (D. Fenner, *personal communication*).

## 4.2. Crown-of-Thorns Starfish Outbreak

The crown-of-thorns starfish *Acanthaster planci* ("alamea" in the Samoan language), preys on coral (Fig. 4.2). Usually, these starfish are a rare member of the reef community; however, plagues of crown-of-thorns starfish can occur rapidly and kill large tracts of coral. The reason

**Figure 4.2. Crown-of-thorns starfish in American Samoa. Photo Credit: Doug Fenner.**

for these outbreaks is still subject to scientific controversy; however, several theories have been proposed. Birkeland (1982) suggests that crown-of-thorns outbreaks occur several years after a heavy rain follows a period of drought. Studies indicate that heavy rains can cause excess nutrient runoff which can fuel plankton blooms that provide food for crown-of-thorns. More larvae survive due to more food and settle into holes in the reef where they feed on coralline algae before finally emerging in daytime after about three years (Birkeland 1982). Brodie et al. (2004) have identified links between increased dissolved inorganic nutrient discharge and crown-of-thorns outbreaks in the Great Barrier Reef. They note that larval development, growth and survival all increased with increased nutrient discharge from rivers. If these theories are correct, than it would follow that more intense storm events associated with climate change could increase nutrient runoff and potentially drive more crown-of-thorns outbreaks in American Samoa.

In 1978 and 1979, an outbreak of crown-of-thorns starfish devastated coral populations on Tutuila's reefs. The massive infestation resulted in a loss of more than 90 percent of all the living corals in Fagatele Bay. At the time, Fagatele Bay was not a Sanctuary, but this disaster helped to propel the decision for the site's designation.

The soft tissues of coral are consumed when crown-of-thorns starfish feeds, leaving behind the hard coral skeleton. As long as other aspects of the ecosystem are intact and new disturbances do not occur, new coral recruitment and growth may replace the damage caused by the starfish. The reefs of Fagatele Bay are resilient because coralline algae rapidly colonizes the dead coral skeletons and cements reef surfaces together to promote the settlement and growth of new coral colonies. Without this rapid colonization by coralline algae, wave action can cause the dead coral skeletons to fragment and turn to rubble before the new coral community can establish. Continued pressure from human impacts coupled with the addition of climate change stressors may decrease the resilience of coral reefs in Fagatele Bay to recover from crown-of-thorns outbreaks.

### 4.3. Agriculture

Agriculture in American Samoa is still largely a subsistence sector with mostly traditional staple food crops, taro, bananas, breadfruit, chickens and pigs. The 1999 Agriculture Census of American Samoa reported that about 41 percent of the territorial land area was being farmed, and nearly 6,500 farms were reported with an average farm size of about three acres. Of these, about 1,100 were classified as commercial operations. A farm was defined as any place that raised or produced any agricultural products for sale or consumption. Approximately 75 percent of households in American Samoa fit this description.

**Figure 4.3. Local landowners grown crops including taro and bananas on the ridge about Fagatele Bay National Marine Sanctuary. Photo Credit: Emily Gaskin.**

With two-thirds of American Samoa's 197 square kilometers having slopes greater than 30 percent and a rainfall of up to 5,000 mm per year, soil erosion is a constant threat. Clearing of land for agriculture within watersheds often decreases the ability of soils to absorb rainfall. Without proper land management, streams carry eroded soils, fertilizers and pesticides into near shore waters. The developed watersheds around Tutuila generally discharge higher sediment loads than undeveloped areas. The steep topography of Fagatele Bay's watershed is particularly vulnerable to erosion once the land is cleared. More intense storm events associated with climate change may increase runoff from farms on the land surrounding Fagatele Bay. (Keller et al. 2008).

Agricultural runoff can decrease the health of Fagatele Bay and reduce resilience to potential climate change impacts. Soil and sediment runoff may impact water quality, habitat integrity and the biological health of the ecosystem. It has also been shown that runoff may exacerbate the impacts of climate change. For example, the combined effect of high sea surface temperatures and sedimentation has been shown to cause coral bleaching (Keller et al. 2008).

## 4.4. Visitation

There is relatively little tourism in American Samoa and it is likely to be some years before the territory enters the mainstream of South Pacific tourism. The annual number of visitors to the National Park of American Samoa ranged from a high of 6,774 in 2007 to a low of 1,239 in 2006 (FBNMS Draft Management Plan/DEIS, 2011). About half of these tourists use marine areas of the park for swimming, snorkeling, or scuba diving. There are also few pleasure boats, about 30 that anchor in Pago Pago Harbor during the cyclone season, but none are found elsewhere in the territory. Tournaments for pelagic sport fish (e.g., tuna, marlin, etc.) occur sporadically, with some 20 small local vessels competing to catch the largest fish (Craig et al. 2005). Visiting Fagatele Bay National Marine Sanctuary is difficult even in good weather due to its remote location and the nature of the terrain that surrounds the bay. Because the land is privately owned, permission is also needed from the landowners to access the bay by land. Little is known about the number of people who visit the bay on a daily basis, but official patrols and visits by sanctuary staff over the past 18 years indicate those numbers are very low. In 2007, a trail was cleared that led from the ridge down to a beach adjacent to the bay, which may have increased visitation. In 2010, the landowners began to ask visitors to sign in before they visited the bay. The sign in sheets indicate that 297 people visited the bay in 2010.

Figure 4.4. Visitors hike to Fagatele Bay National Marine Sanctuary. Photo Credit: Veronika Mortenson.

There are few locally owned pleasure boats in American Samoa. Yachts come to Pago Pago Harbor to buy provisions and find shelter during the cyclone season. Sportfishing for pelagic tuna, mahi mahi, and marlin is popular and occasional fishing tournaments are held, but these activities occur in offshore waters rather than on the coastal reefs. There are no commercial SCUBA diving operators presently in the territory, but the potential to attract sport divers to Fagatele Bay and the territory's coral reefs exists. Despite the low numbers of visitors, human impacts on coral reefs surrounding Tutuila Island, including Fagatele Bay, have the potential to be severe. Documented impacts due to visitation of the bay include: unregulated fishing, illegal collection of corals and other invertebrates, and damage to the reef from boat anchors and walking on the reef flat. Anchor damage has been observed, and in response, two mooring buoys were installed in 2006 to allow boaters to visit the bay without dropping anchor. Discarded trash is also a potential problem caused by both land and sea visitors to the bay. Together these human impacts have the potential to decrease the resilience of coral reef ecosystems. Therefore, it is important that managers continue to regulate use for all users wishing to visit the site.

# 5. Impacts on the Human Environment

## 5.1. Impacts to Society/Economic Sectors

The potential impacts of climate change to society and economic sectors in American Samoa could be significant. Sea level rise, increased sea surface temperatures, ocean acidification, and extreme weather events will impact natural systems, physical infrastructure, and human capital that support lives and livelihoods. Shifting species distribution, range, and abundance could have serious consequences for the local subsistence and commercial fishing communities. Coral bleaching and coastal erosion could discourage recreation activities including snorkeling and diving. Shoreline erosion and coastal flooding could force local residents onto increasingly marginal lands on steeper slopes. In extreme cases, climate change impacts may jeopardize human security and even the survival of pacific islands (Lal et al. 2009).

The potential impacts of climate change to human livelihoods are challenging and complex. Furthermore, assessments of the potential social and economic costs of climate change in American Samoa and the Pacific region are limited and partial. Recently economic impact assessments have been conducted to evaluate the costs of past natural disasters in several Pacific Island nations including Fiji and Vanuatu. Other studies have applied disaggregated techniques to evaluate the physical impacts of climate related disasters and economic models to assess impacts to various economic sectors. In 2009 the Secretariat of the Pacific Regional Environment Program (SPREP) published a review of the economic and livelihood impacts of climate change in Melanesia. The study applied both quantitative and qualitative research methods including modeling, empirical judgment, expert judgment and anecdotal evidence, to evaluate the economic costs of climate change in the Pacific (Lal et al. 2009).

In 2010, the World Bank evaluated the potential costs of adaptation to climate change in Samoa using a benefits transfer approach. The study estimated the costs of investing in adaptation planning to ensure that new or upgraded assets could withstand potential climate impacts including sea level rise, higher wind speeds, and increased cyclone intensity (World Bank 2010). The Asian Development Bank (ADB) is currently undertaking a project to evaluate the economics of climate change in the Pacific however at the time of this publication the draft report has not been released (P. Holland, *personal communication*).

## 5.1.1. Economic Costs of Climate Change

The economic costs of climate change in American Samoa will depend on the nature of the event as well as the sensitivity of the natural environment and coping capacity (Lal et al. 2009). In general, smaller economies are more vulnerable to external climate shocks because they often rely on few economic activities (IPCC 2007). Island economies are also particularly vulnerable to climate change events because islands have limited natural resources and are often dependent on imports. Without additional adaptation, the present value of climate impacts to the Samoan economy through 2050 was estimated to be $104-$212 million or 0.6-1.3% of the present value of GDP of the Samoan economy (World Bank 2010).[1] Preliminary findings from the ADB study

---

[1] The study chose two climate models, the Commonwealth Scientific and Industrial Research Organization (CSIRO) and the National Center for Atmospheric Research (NCAR), to capture a wide range predictions.

suggest that without global mitigation of greenhouse gas emissions or regional adaptation, the South Pacific could lose an equivalent of 12% of GDP by 2100 (Suphachalasai 2010).[2] Furthermore, if current emissions trends continue, the Pacific may require up to $300 million per year (1% of GDP) to cope with climate change (Suphachalasai 2010).

In American Samoa, local residents have expressed concern about the potential economic effects of climate change. In a recent study, over 80% of the residents in the villages of Amouli and Ofu indicated that they believe that climate change events will impact the economy (Wongbusarakum 2010). Fagatele Bay National Marine Sanctuary is currently conducting a similar study of community vulnerability and adaptive capacity with respect to climate change on the island of Aunu'u off the east coast of Tutuila. The results of the study will be used to inform locally appropriate and relevant adaptation strategies.

### 5.1.2. Goods and Services

**Figure 5.1. The coral reef ecosystem in Fagatele Bay National Marine Sanctuary provides essential goods and services. Photo Credit: NOAA CRED.**

Coral reef ecosystems provide essential goods and services to the people of American Samoa including coastal protection, waste assimilation, research, recreation, and education (Spurgeon et al. 2004). Goods and services from coral reef ecosystems could be threatened by potential climate change impacts. Increased sea surface temperature and changing ocean circulation patterns could impact species distribution, range and abundance among other things. Coral bleaching and ocean acidification could also threaten the availability of goods and services from coral reef ecosystems.

The coral reefs of American Samoa provide benefits to both the territory and the mainland. Total direct and indirect use benefits of coral reefs to American Samoa residents and visitors are estimated to be worth around $1.28 million per year (Spurgeon et al. 2004).  When potential non-use benefits accruing to U.S. citizens are included, overall benefits of coral reefs could be at least $10 million per year. Overall non-use values are around $8.8 million per year (87% of the total economic value). Non-use values include the beauty or aesthetic value of the reef, the potential value to future generations (bequest value), and the value in knowing the reef exists (existence value). The use value for coral reefs to American Samoa is relatively low compared with American Samoa's annual Gross Domestic Product, because tourism and recreational access to corals are limited. Extensive man-made shoreline defenses, which have been constructed for beach sand and rubble mining, and the relatively poor and small population, have contributed to this low recreation and tourism value. Excluding the U.S. public non-use values, the combined annual coral value is only around 1% of American Samoa's annual Gross Domestic Product (Spurgeon et al. 2004 in FBNMS Draft Management Plan/DEIS, 2011).

---

[2] The study was based on certain assumptions including an average mean temperature change of 4.6°C by 2100 and a predicted sea level rise of 70 cm on average (with an upper limit of 1.5-2.0 m).

### 5.1.3. Subsistence Fishing

Subsistence fishing occurs at a small scale in American Samoa using small boats and traditional fishing techniques for consumption mainly by the family and community (FBNMS Draft Management Plan/DEIS, 2011). Subsistence fishing is relatively common in American Samoa however it has declined over the last 30 years with the shift towards a cash-based economy (Wass 1980). Subsistence fishermen primarily catch jacks, surgeonfish, mullet, groupers, snappers, squirrelfish, parrotfish, lobster, octopus, sea urchins, bivalves, and various gastropods (Saucerman 1995). Total annual fish catch in American Samoa is approximately 104 tons per year (Coutures 2003, Spurgeon et al. 2004). Based on the average retail market prices for similar fish traded on the market

**Figure 5.2. Reef fish harvested in the waters around American Samoa.**

in 2004, the value of subsistence catch in American Samoa was determined to be approximately $572,000 per year (Spurgeon et al. 2004).[3] Subsistence consumer surplus, defined as the benefit to residents from fishing, was estimated to be an additional $73,000 per year. Climate change impacts could reduce the available catch for subsistence fisherman in American Samoa. Climate variability can have a significant effect on recruitment of fish populations (Cushing 1995). Ocean acidification studies have found deleterious impacts of acidification on fish and their larvae. Human exploitation of coral reef resources may further exacerbate the effects of climate change on fish populations (see 4.2.4: "Fish" section).

### 5.1.4. Commercial Fishing

The coral reef commercial fishing industry has declined in American Samoa over the last century with the introduction of new alternative industries. Local resource agencies believe that a ban on SCUBA fishing has resulted in a subsequent decline in fish entering the marketplace (DMWR 2002). However, commercial fishing for coral reef products is still practiced in many villages throughout the territory. In American Samoa approximately 3.1% of the population is employed in agriculture, forestry, fishing, hunting, and mining (information was not available for fishing only; FBNMS Draft Management Plan/DEIS 2011). In 2004 the market value of coral reef products

**Figure 5.3. A Japanese long line fishing vessel at dock in Pago Pago harbor in 1962. Long lining has replaced other forms of fishing because it is more profitable. Photo Credit: NOAA.**

---

[3] A multiplier effect can account for additional indirect and induced expenditures (i.e. fishing and diving). This figure includes a multiplier effect of 1.25.

extracted in American Samoa was estimated to be around $30,000 per year for reef fish and $14,000 per year for lobster. It is not believed that commercial fish is regularly practiced in Fagatele Bay; however the sanctuary's remote location makes enforcement of regulations difficult.

As discussed in the previous section, climate variability and ocean acidification, coupled with human exploitation, could result in declining reef fish populations in American Samoa (see 4.2.4: "Fish" section). In Samoa the estimated economic impact to fisheries (near-shore and pelagic) from climate change was calculated as the compensation required to offset the reduction in value-added generated by fishing in Samoa's Exclusive Economic Zone (World Bank 2010). The present value of the costs of climate impacts to the fisheries sector through 2050 was determined to be approximately $3.1 million per year.

### 5.1.5.  Recreation Tourism

Coral reef ecosystems provide local residents and tourists with recreation opportunities. However tourism has decreased considerably in American Samoa over the past fifty years. The number of tourists visiting American Samoa has decreased from an average of 35,000 per year in the 1970s to 6,126 in 2010 with the trend continuing to decrease (DOC 2011). Currently tourism only contributes 7% to the local economy. It is unlikely that many visitors come to American Samoa specifically for coral reefs but they may play a role in attracting tourists (Spurgeon et al. 2004). As discussed in chapter 5 of this document, visiting Fagatele Bay National Marine Sanctuary is difficult even in good weather due to its remote location and the nature of the terrain that surrounds the bay. However local residents and tourists do visit the bay to snorkel and less frequently to dive. In 2010 approximately 297 individuals visited Fagatele Bay.

**Figure 5.4. In 2011 eleven cruise ships will visit America Samoa. Visitors enjoy snorkeling the coral reefs around American Samoa. Photo Credit: Doug Fenner.**

Climate impacts could further reduce the limited number of visitors to American Samoa and FBNMS. Visitors depend on certain variables including good weather, clean beaches, and healthy coral reefs when they select a vacation destination. Climate induced changes to natural resources including coastal erosion and coral reef degradation could deter visitors. An IPCC Working Group survey determined that 80% of tourists would not wish to return to a bleached coral area (IPCC 2007). An increase in the frequency and intensity of extreme weather events could also discourage visitors as well as threaten basic infrastructure for visitors.

As a result of low levels of tourism and low participation in recreational activities by local residents, the recreational value of coral reefs in American Samoa is extremely low relative to the recreational value of coral reefs at other locations in the Pacific and globally. Often the recreation value of coral reefs represents a significant part of the total economic value of the coral reef. For example a travel cost study on the total economic value of coral reefs globally found that recreation and tourism value is approximately $3,008 per hectare per year or approximately half of their total value (Costanza et al. 1997). [4] In Moorea, the island in French Polynesia with the most tourism activity, the economic value of coral reefs from tourism was estimated to be approximately $15,320 per hectare per year and contributes to 90% of the total reef value of $17,100 per hectare per year (Charles 2005). In American Samoa recreation value only represents 0.7% of the total economic value of coral reefs. The extremely low recreational value of coral reefs in American Samoa may mislead decision makers who are looking to invest in coral reefs with high total economic value. It is important to consider that the methodology used to estimate the total economic value of coral reefs is skewed heavily towards variables that can be easily measured such as recreation and tourism and omits variables that may not be as easily quantified such as cultural value, aesthetic value, and existence value.

### 5.1.5.1. Snorkeling

Climate impacts could reduce the number of snorkelers in American Samoa. There are many conditions that limit recreational snorkeling in American Samoa including difficulties in accessing good snorkeling areas due to the fringing reefs, dangerous swimming conditions due to high wave action and rip currents, permission needed by owners of the foreshore before one can swim, and the paucity of equipment, facilities and information about sites (Spurgeon et al. 2004). However there are several protected areas that provide ideal snorkeling conditions, including the sanctuary. An informal survey conducted in 2004 determined that approximately 2,750 snorkel trips occur in American Samoa per year (Spurgeon et al. 2004).

**Figure 5.5. 2011 Snorkeler in Fagatele Bay National Marine Sanctuary. Photo Credit: Victoria Szlag.**

The average snorkeling related expenditure for transport, food, and travel is estimated to be $10 for tourists and $4 for residents, or $20,000 per year. [5]

Recreation consumer surplus is defined as the benefit from enjoyment gained from a recreational activity (in this case snorkeling). Similar studies conducted in Florida and Hawaii determined that the recreation consumer surplus of snorkeling is approximately $12 per person per trip (Cesar et al. 2002, NOAA 2004). In American Samoa consumer surplus was estimated to be $4 per person per trip because of a lack of substitute activities and the fact that most resident snorkelers are Caucasian (Spurgeon et al. 2004). Based on these assumptions the total annual recreation consumer surplus for snorkeling was estimated to be approximately $45,000 per year and the expenditures are estimated to be $20,000 per year. [6]

---

[4] Travel cost estimates a visitor's willingness to pay based on travel time and travel costs associated with visiting a certain site.

[5] Expenditures were converted to expenditure added values by subtracting costs of production. The costs are assumed to be 75% of expenditures in the tourism sector based on Cesar et al. (2002). This figure includes a multiplier effect of 1.25.

### 5.1.5.2. Diving

Climate impacts could also reduce the number of divers in American Samoa. Currently, there is very limited recreational diving in the territory. There are currently no commercial dive outlets in the territory. In the past, two dive outlets existed, but received most of their trade from visiting research scientists and were therefore not considered for recreational diving values (Spurgeon et al. 2004). Most of the business of the last surviving dive shop was to fill tanks for scuba spear fishing, but the store closed following the ban on scuba spear fishing. Although no formal studies have been conducted, it has been estimated that there are approximately 15 active divers who reside in American Samoa who each complete approximately 30 dives per year for a total of 450 dives. An average consumer surplus value of $10 per dive was assumed for residents and $20 for visitors (Spurgeon et al. 2004). These consumer surplus values are relatively low compared to other comparable dive sites for residents because they complete dives multiple times throughout the year and for tourists because they have to pay a significant sum to go diving. Recreation related expenditure added value is the economic impact of direct and indirect activities related to the activity. Average dive related

**Figure 5.6. Diver at Swains Island, American Samoa. Photo Credit: Jim Nimz, National Park of American Samoa.**

expenditure added value including food, equipment and boat costs are estimated to be $10 for residents and $90 for tourists (Spurgeon et al. 2004). Based on the above assumptions the total annual dive consumer surplus is estimated to be around $5,000 per year and expenditure of just under $3,000 per year.

### 5.1.6. Shoreline Protection

**Figure 5.7. Coastal erosion at Lyon's Park, Tafuna, American Samoa. Photo Credit: Doug Fenner.**

Coral reefs protect shoreline infrastructure such as buildings and roads from waves and storm surges. The overall benefit from coral reefs with respect to shoreline protection in American Samoa has been valued at approximately $447,000 per year (Spurgeon et al. 2004). However this figure may be very conservative as much of the shoreline protection function is provided by the solid limestone reef matrix laid down over thousands of years that, in many locations, has relatively low coral cover (Spurgeon et al. 2004). The costs of coastal protection for Samoa were estimated to be approximately $40,000 per year using the dynamic and interactive vulnerability assessment (DIVA) under a high sea level rise scenario (World Bank 2010). A majority of the costs were required to upgrade the port in the capital city Apia. The study also found that during the decade 2040-2049, an average of 170 people per year will be affected by climate change under a high sea level rise scenario.

An increase in the frequency and intensity of tropical cyclones may damage fragile coastal reefs and result in the flooding and erosion of low-lying coastal areas. Wave energy attenuation over the outer reef flat has been measured on various Caribbean and Pacific reefs to be between 75% and 95% (Roberts et al. 1992). Rising sea levels would allow more wave energy to reach shore if the reef did not grow upward at the same rate that sea level rose. The ability of the reef to attenuate wave power depends on the water depth on the reef flat. The deeper it is, the less energy the reef can absorb. The greatest damage to shorelines will occur with the largest waves, which will be in hurricanes. For the near future, the reef can keep up with sea level rise, but in future decades when higher water temperatures cause mass coral bleaching and mass coral deaths, the reef will likely not be able to keep up, and eventually shoreline erosion will increase. The power of the waves to erode the shoreline can easily be seen east of Pago Pago harbor where many black basalt rocks torn out of the shoreline litter the reef flat (D. Fenner, *personal communication*).

**Figure 5.8. Sea wall in front of Vatia village on the north shore of Tutuila, American Samoa. Photo Credit: Doug Fenner.**

American Samoa is particularly vulnerable to coastal erosion because the relatively narrow fringing reefs that surround the islands limit the reef area available for carbonate sediment production. Furthermore, American Samoa has little flat land making land erosion a significant threat. Most roads and villages are located along the coast and relocation is often not possible or desirable especially given that family are often buried in garden plots on the shoreline (Spurgeon et al. 2004). Some of the land in villages was actually built by dredging material from reef flats, such as in Alofau, Faga'alu, Aua and Gataivai. The airport runway was built on reef flats and built up by dredging reef flat on both sides of the runway. In addition, some reefs in the harbor were filled in and built on, for instance the Rainmaker Hotel was build on reef flat next to "Goat Island."

## 5.2. Maritime Heritage

In addition to the critical roles of marine species and marine ecosystems, our oceans and coastlines also hold another special resource, one inextricably linked to human society. They hold the physical records of our own seafaring and maritime past. These take the form of cultural, archaeological, and historical properties or locations, which are referred to collectively as maritime heritage resources. NOAA's Office of National Marine Sanctuaries is committed to preserving maritime heritage resources within the sanctuary system and within federally controlled waters. Significant heritage resources fall under the management and protection of established state and federal preservation laws.

## 5.2.1. Maritime Heritage as Marine Resource

**Figure 5.9. Shipwreck on the southeast side of Tutuila. Photo Credit: NOAA.**

Like natural resources, maritime heritage resources may be affected by climatic change in the short, medium, and long term. Such effects may differ in magnitude when compared to broad climate impacts on large-scale natural ecosystems, but depending on the location and character of the resource, significant damage to or complete loss of cultural properties can occur. Therefore, it is important to consider the possible impacts to these special and non-renewable resources.

Heritage resources can possess sufficient historical and/or archaeological significance and information to warrant protection and preservation in their own right. However, when it comes to certain resources such as coastal human habitation sites, these heritage resources may contain information directly related to long- term climate change. Both the physical content (floral/faunal remains) and the specific location (more recently inundated or exposed) can provide evidence directly related to past ocean levels and climatic regimes. It is critical to not only understand possible impacts, but to protect certain resources as well.

Assessing these potential impacts in American Samoa is difficult, for field surveys of coastal archaeological and historical sites have been limited, and underwater surveys of maritime heritage resources have not yet been conducted. Given the scarcity of data from the field, the following can only describe in very general terms the kinds of impacts that climatic change *may* have to the types of maritime heritage resources expected to be found in American Samoa.

## 5.2.2. Maritime Heritage in American Samoa

A preliminary document-based inventory of maritime heritage resources was initiated by the Office of National Marine Sanctuaries in 2007 using existing published material and other accessible records (Van Tilburg 2007). Most identified coastal and submerged maritime heritage resources fall into a number of categories:

1. Historic western shipwrecks lost in American Samoa: There are 39 reported ship losses, 10 of which are identified historic vessels known to have gone missing in American Samoan waters, the earliest dating to 1828. This may only represent a portion of a larger resource base. These vessels link the islands to British colonization efforts in the Pacific, to whaling heritage, and to naval activities in World War II. Except for the USS *Chehalis* in Pago Pago Harbor, none of these wreck sites have been located.

2. World War II naval aircraft lost in American Samoa: Forty-three naval aircraft are reported as having ditched or crashed into American Samoan waters between 1942 and 1944, principally in the vicinity of Tutuila. Some of these sites may be war graves; all remain property of the U.S. Government, and are protected by the Federal Sunken Military Craft Act (2005), as are any military shipwrecks. None of the aircraft have been located.

3. World War II fortifications, gun emplacements, and coastal pillboxes: A wide assortment of naval defensive structures provides the more visible heritage of the World War II period in American Samoa. They are a testimony to the important military role of the islands during a pivotal period in the region's history. Joseph Kennedy, principal investigator with Archaeological Consultants of the Pacific Inc., recently completed a separate inventory of all World War II coastal defense structures on Tutuila Island documenting 132 coastal sites, many being impacted by coastal erosion (Kennedy 2005).

4. Coastal archaeological sites associated with the ancient past: Samoan archaeological artifacts and sites associated with the marine and coastal setting include: pottery, whet stones or grinding stones (*foaga*), petroglyphs, grinding holes/bait cups, lithic scatters (stone tool manufacture) and stratified cultural layers related to habitation sites. These sites record critical information about the ancient past. Currently 21 sites are listed in the ONMS inventory, but more research is needed. Field data from numerous surveys exists at the American Samoa Community College and the American Samoa Historic Preservation Office.

5. Marine/coastal natural resources associated with folklore: In Samoa, natural features such as coastal rocks or caves or beaches (Palagi Beach is said to be haunted) can be associated with beliefs which are rooted in the community's history and are critical in maintaining cultural identity. These locations, featured in legends and myths, are visible touchstones of oral history. These sites "are of extraordinary significance to Samoan culture. Compared to all of the archaeological and historic sites that the HPO [Historic Preservation Office] tries to protect, these sites are seen as the most significant to local residents." (Volk et al. 1992) There are 20 such sites listed in the inventory. Locations which help maintain cultural identity may have great social importance in the face of climate-driven cultural change (see also Samoan Studies Institute 2009).

The following projections are based on a summary review of estimated climate change drivers, including increased acidification, increased temperature and salinity, stronger and more frequent cyclonic storm events, and rising ocean levels.

### 5.2.3. Short Term Changes to Sites (event-driven)

Short- term events such as tropical cyclones, storm surges, and tsunamis are capable of producing immediate and serious damage. Coastal resources such as ancient Samoan archaeological sites and natural features associated with Samoan cultural history and legends may be particularly vulnerable as many are located in the high-energy coastal impact zone. Likewise, historic World War II pillboxes line the immediate coast in close proximity to rising sea levels. Even large steel shipwrecks located at 30 m depth may be moved or broken by major storm events, as has been demonstrated in the Florida Keys (B. Altmeier, *personal communication*, 10/21/10).

Increased coastal erosion due to climatic change is already suspected in places like Barrow, Alaska, where the lack of coast ice has exposed the shoreline to increased erosion, damaging ancient Inupiat burial and village sites (Christiansen 2010). New GIS tools are providing the means to prioritize threatened archaeological sites on the Georgia coast (Robinson et al. 2010). Information on wave action, coastal slope and shoreline geomorphology, and historic shoreline change rates can be combined to provide an accurate assessment of archaeological site vulnerability (Reeder et al. 2010). A survey of coastal archaeological sites and artifacts exposed by the 29 September 2009 tsunami in American Samoa has been conducted (Addison et al. 2010). Fifty new lithic sites were exposed and damaged by the destructive waves, which reached over 17 m in height at some locations. These cultural layers near the shore may contain abundant archaeological material for understanding past climate regimes.

### 5.2.4.  Medium Term Changes to Sites (1-10 years)

Wood has provided material for thousands of years of boat building. Wooden heritage resources include canoes, boats, and ships, and wooden artifacts associated with coastal archaeological sites. Wood is more ephemeral than metal, subject to mechanical and biological degradation in a matter of years rather than decades. Mechanical weathering sources include ocean currents, swells and sediment abrasion. Biological deterioration follows from bacteria and other marine organisms attacking the cell structure of the cellulose, allowing the wood to become "water-logged." In temperate to warm marine environments, the ship worm *Teredo navalis* may be responsible for the majority of the destruction of exposed wooden ship remains. Only where components are buried in sediment or otherwise protected by an anaerobic environment, do wooden artifacts remain intact. Where climatic change may be extending the range of the ship worm, as in the Baltic Sea, thousands of intact historic shipwrecks are now being threatened (University of Gothenburg 2010). However, conditions for the ship worm already exist throughout the Samoan Islands. Therefore, any existing wooden artifacts likely remain buried in sediments and protected. Climate changes, which alter circulation and remove sediments, may expose these wooden remains to greater deterioration.

### 5.2.5.  Long Term Changes to Sites (10-100 years)

Heritage sites like historic shipwrecks or submerged aircraft, following the initial deposition or wrecking event, tend towards greater equilibrium or stability in certain environments. For sites protected either by depth or otherwise sheltered from surface storm impacts, the slower bio-chemical processes of material deterioration dominate the long-term changes to the site's condition. Heritage properties can include a wide variety of materials, such as lead, ceramics, glass, stone, aluminum, bone, etc. These react differently in the marine environment. However, the large majority of submerged historic sites are characterized predominantly by wood, iron/steel, and/or copper.

Iron may be the most plentiful and functional metal used by humans, and is often found at maritime heritage sites (Rodgers 2004). In the marine environment, iron and ferrous metals undergo both corrosion and concretion processes. Corrosion is a process where iron, in contact with water and oxygen, will lose iron ions and produce ferrous oxy-hydroxide, also known as "rust". Dissolved salts increase conductivity, enhancing the electrochemical corrosion process (Overfield

**Figure 5.10. Bronze pintle (ship's rudder hardware) from the British whaling vessel *Pearl*, lost in 1822. Sand scouring marks reveal abrasion of the relatively soft metal below the initial exposed surface. Photo Credit: ONMS photographer H. Van Tilburg. ONMS.**

2005). Therefore, relatively long term climate changes which increase salinity may have the effect of slightly increasing the rate of the corrosion process on ferrous metals, though it is unknown whether this slight theoretical increase would be measurable. The corrosion process can be slowed where impermeable barriers exist between iron and sea water (though some corrosion can continue due to the action of sulphate-reducing bacteria in the anaerobic environment; Heldtberg et al. 2004). The formation of concretions on ferrous metals follows a progression of bio-fouling assemblages, then coralline algae, then layers of hard coral (calcium carbonate), leading to a fairly impervious encrustation. This layer not only slows the corrosion process, but also helps protect the wreck from sediment scour and storm surge action (Overfield 2005). Therefore, climatic changes which increase acidification and reduce calcification rates could reduce concretion on iron artifacts, potentially increasing wreck corrosion. However, our ability to measure this slight change over the long term remains unknown.

Copper and cupreous (containing copper) metals, very useful in a variety of nautical applications such as fasteners, hull sheathing, and ships' hardware, are slightly toxic to marine species and therefore do not undergo the same protective concretion processes of iron. Fortunately, copper is electrically passive, and does not suffer the relatively fast corrosion processes of iron. Cupreous artifacts may survive for hundreds of years in the marine environment. The relatively soft metal, though, is subject to mechanical weathering of scouring and abrasion (Fig. 5.9). Thus, copper and bronze artifacts can also be affected in the medium term by changes in sediment transport and the mechanical processes of scouring and abrasion.

### 5.2.6.  Challenges to Understanding Climatic Change and Maritime Heritage

Maritime heritage resources are intertwined with the natural environment; there are multiple relationships between the heritage resource and the biological ecosystem, some beneficial, some detrimental. Neither the heritage resource nor the natural ecosystem can truly be understood in isolation from one another. Understanding these relationships, and the role that climatic change might play, is challenging for the following reasons:

1.  Finding the "signal" through the "noise": Determining the direct link between climate change and the condition of maritime heritage resources may be difficult at best, for some of these non-renewable resources are continually influenced by a number of environmental and cultural factors. The factors that shape the archaeological site, such as winds, depth, current, sediment type,  along with all cultural influences, such as salvage and site excavation, fall under the single category of post-depositional "site formation processes" (Muckelroy 1978). Understanding the cumulative effect of these processes plays a central role in interpreting the nature and distribution of the submerged site (Fig. 5.10).

2.  Lack of data: The only existing resource inventory for American Samoa is based on historical documents, not field survey. Such historical records are vague about specific positions. Furthermore, each shipwreck, aircraft or archaeological site has changed over the years due to site formation processes. The specific location and current actual condition of heritage resources in American Samoa is unknown. Additionally, beyond the existing descriptions of how archaeological wood, iron, copper, glass etc. react in a *generalized* marine environment (Pearson 1988, Rodgers 2004), almost no information exists on how resources react in specific environments or locations. The issue may only be addressed on a case-by-case basis,

for there is no *standard* or *generic* shipwreck or archaeological site. Many resources vary in age, date of deposition, construction, material composition and design.

Little is known about the specific condition of most maritime heritage resources in American Samoa, but certain observations can be made regarding the possible effects of climatic change. It may be difficult to isolate climatic change effects on heritage resources in deeper water, due to the rate of that change and the number of other "non-climatic" influences to the resource. Coastal and shallow water sites may likely be impacted to a greater degree from short -term events like storms. Coastal and shallow water areas may, therefore, be regarded as higher priority for the purposes of proposed maritime heritage surveys. Ancient coastal Samoan sites, due to their demonstrated archaeological significance and potential vulnerability to erosion and storm events, may be considered as important heritage resources within potentially affected areas.

Coastal archaeological sites, besides being considered as potentially threatened resources, play an important role in the changing climate story, as mentioned above. Such sites are capable of revealing aspects of not just ancient human behavior, but the nature of past biological and physical environments in previous ocean stands and climatic regimes. In other words, the abundance and variety of floral and faunal remains and the location of the archaeological features themselves provide direct evidence of the ancient environment. Therefore, coastal archaeological sites *must be considered as critical potential indicators of climate change themselves,* as tools measuring previous ocean levels and different climate regimes.

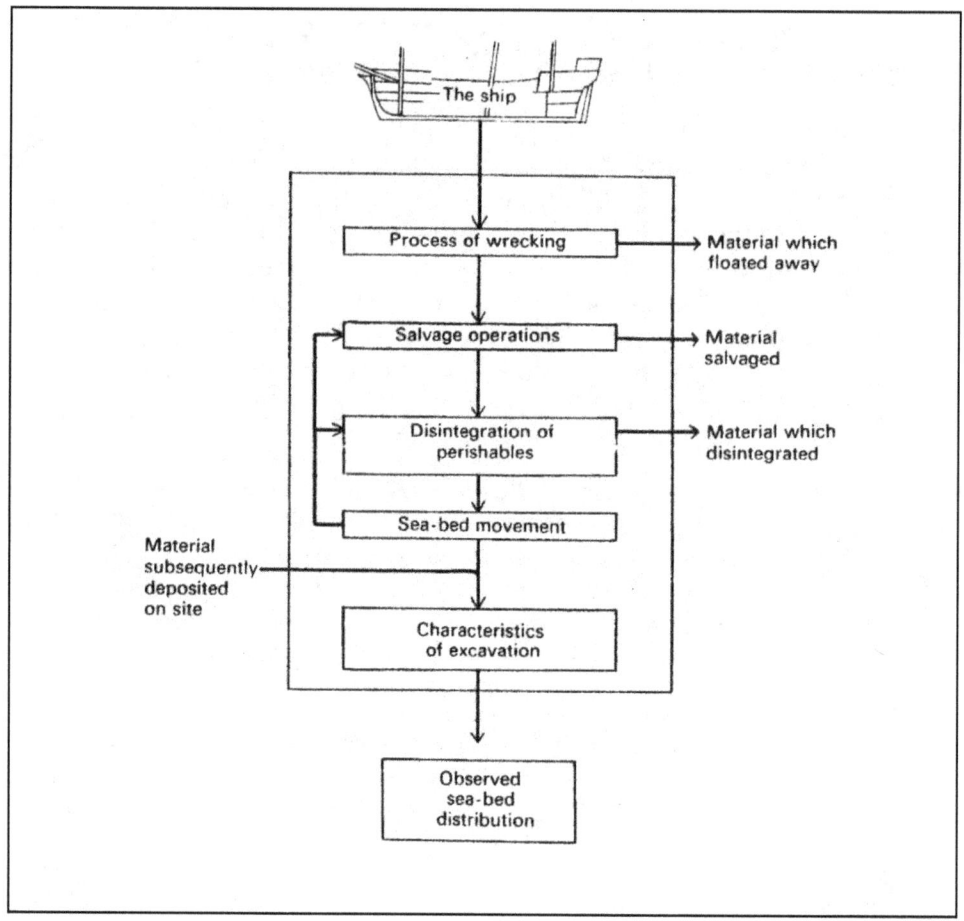

**Figure 5.11. Muckelroy's description of the site formation process, environmental and cultural variables which alter the shipwreck from initial deposition to discovery. (Muckelroy 1978: 158).**

## 6.   Management Response

The Sanctuary will produce a Climate Change Plan as a companion document to this document. The Climate Change Plan will include priority actions for the sanctuary to take in the next five to ten years to respond to the impacts of climate change on human activities and natural systems within the Sanctuary. The priority actions will address climate change impacts identified in the this document, as well as recommendations proposed by community members, coastal resource managers and policy makers in American Samoa.

Priority actions will include both mitigation activities to reduce greenhouse gas emissions into the atmosphere, as well as adaptation activities to tolerate the effects of climate change and ocean acidification. The Climate Change Plan will provide detailed descriptions of each of the activities, as well as the problem area to be addressed and implementation strategies. The plan will note both existing and needed resources including partners, funding expertise, knowledge, and information. The plan will also present a timeline for completing certain specific outcomes and milestones.

A working group will be established to advise the Sanctuary on the development of activities to be included in the Climate Change Plan. The working group will consist of Sanctuary Advisory Council members as well as coastal resource managers and scientists in American Samoa. The working group will meet to review the recommendations proposed by community members, coastal resource managers, and policy makers in American Samoa, and to propose additional activities to address impacts identified in this document. Furthermore, the working group will be asked to review the draft document before it is released to the public.

The Climate Change Plan will build upon existing strategies that inform adaptation activities in American Samoa. In particular, the Climate Change Plan will complement the Climate Change Planning Framework that has been developed by the American Samoa Government to prepare for potential climate change impacts in the territory. The Plan will also build upon the climate change goals and objectives developed by NOAA's Coral Reef Conservation Program. Finally, the Plan will incorporate all priorities and strategies developed and promoted by NOAA's Office of National Marine Sanctuaries.

# 7.  Conclusions

Global climate change may have significant consequences for coral reef ecosystems, coastal communities, and maritime heritage resources relevant to the Fagatele Bay National Marine Sanctuary (FBNMS). However, there are few climate change specific studies that discuss FBNMS and surrounding waters. This paper identifies and synthesizes potential climate change impacts in American Samoa and the region.  The key physical drivers include climate variability (including extreme events), sea surface warming, ocean acidification, and sea level rise.

Climate variability and the occurrence of extreme weather events can have significant impacts on marine communities and cultural resources within American Samoa and FBNMS. These may manifest as intense tropical cyclones, as periods of high precipitation followed by drought, or other anomalous climate conditions. Natural variation in climate (e.g. PDO, ENSO) not only increases the difficulty of detecting trends in data but it also has the potential to intensify or ameliorate climate change impacts depending on the phase of the cycle. Surface warming will also have large impacts on organism physiology and other physical processes such as water column stratification and the subsequent effects on nutrient supply. Lastly, the impacts of increased atmospheric carbon dioxide and its dissolution in ocean waters cannot be underestimated. Many physiological processes are dependent on ocean chemistry and alterations to these properties can effect calcification, growth, sensory abilities and other organism processes.

There are also natural and cultural resources that may be of concern when considering climate impacts. Corals are a particularly important group in FBNMS due to their sensitivity to all of the physical drivers discussed in this document. Extreme storm events have the capacity to remove corals in wave exposed areas or increase sedimentation with negative effects on coral photosynthesis. Warming is predicted to cause mass coral bleaching and mass coral mortalities that are predicted to severely degrade the coral reef to the point that it would no longer be called a coral reef, but rather an algae bed. This may also result in coral disease outbreaks that commonly follow mass coral bleaching and which can cause more coral mortality than the bleaching event itself. It may also facilitate disease in corals, during non-bleaching periods and ocean acidification which are predicted to inhibit the formation of calcium carbonate skeletons. Corals are a key species not only because they are potentially susceptible to many climate drivers, but also because they create additional complex habitat that is utilized by a diversity of marine fish and invertebrates.

Several other groups emerge as important species of concern in addition to corals. Calcareous algae, most notably the encrusting corallines play an important role in the settlement of coral larvae, as well as a critical role in building the reef and cementing the reef crest well enough to keep it from being destroyed by waves. This group is more sensitive to ocean acidification that will slow calcium carbonate deposition because it deposits calcite which dissolves more readily. Other marine calcifying invertebrates such as echinoderms, mollusks, and crustaceans will also be affected. Climate change may also modify the activity of primary producers such as phytoplankton with cascading effects on species that are dependent on this production such as zooplankton, reef and pelagic invertebrates and fishes. In addition to the direct effects of climate change on marine populations, climate change can have indirect effects on organisms by potentially favoring conditions for invasive species, disease, or other species that have a strong effect on the ecosystem (e.g. crown-of-thorns starfish).

Changing climate conditions could significantly impact coastal communities and human livelihoods in relevant to FBNMS in American Samoa. Sea level rise, increased sea surface temperatures, ocean acidification, and extreme weather events will impact natural systems, physical infrastructure, and human capital that support lives and livelihoods. Shifting species distribution, range, and abundance could have serious consequences for the local subsistence and commercial fishing communities. Coral bleaching and coastal erosion could discourage recreation activities including snorkeling and diving. Shoreline erosion and coastal flooding could force local residents onto increasingly marginal lands on steeper slopes.

Knowledge of cultural resources within American Samoa and FBNMS is limited. However, coastal and shallow water areas may be particularly sensitive to impacts from sea level rise and extreme storm activity. Ancient coastal Samoan sites, for example, have an inherent archaeological significance to the region and are vulnerable to the physical drivers as well as erosion. These sites are important not only because of their cultural significance but also because they may be used as indicators of past environmental conditions.

Predictions of physical climate change and biological responses to these drivers are difficult at best. Some studies have also suggested that the effects of climate change on Earth will be largely irreversible if action is not taken swiftly in the near future. Current levels of greenhouse gases have already probably committed the global system to some kinds of change, such as sea level rise and greater temperatures that are estimated to persist for at least 1000 years. Attenuation of climate impacts may be an effective strategy for coping with change. This may require (i) identifying vulnerable or important resources for management and (ii) ameliorating non-climate stressors (e.g. extraction pressure, pollution, invasive species, etc.). Further discussion of potential management actions will reside within the Fagatele Bay National Marine Sanctuary Climate Change Plan.

# Glossary

**Accretion**: the accumulation of sediment, deposited by natural fluid flow processes.

**Alamea:** Samoan word for crown-of-thorns starfish, *Acanthaster planci*.

**Amplitude**: the magnitude of change in a wave; one half the wave height.

**Anthropogenic**: effects, processes or materials derived from human activities

**Aragonite**: a carbonate mineral; one of the two common (the other is calcite) naturally occurring polymorphs of calcium carbonate.

**Benefit Transfer:** environmental valuation technique that uses the transfer of economic values estimated in one context and location in order to estimate values in a similar or different context and location. The values should ideally be adjusted based on key criteria and variations that apply in the different contexts and locations. This technique is used when it is not feasible to carry out primary data collection.

**Biodiversity:** the variation of life forms within a given ecosystem, biome, or for the entire Earth.

**Bottom-up:** nutrient supply and productivity and type of primary producers (plants and phytoplankton) are controlling the ecosystem structure.

**Calcite:** the most stable polymorph of calcium carbonate, one of the two common naturally occurring polymorphs of calcium carbonate (the other is aragonite).

**Carbon cycle:** the biogeochemical cycle by which carbon is continuously exchanged among Earth's five major reservoirs of carbon (biosphere, pedosphere, geosphere, hydrosphere, and atmosphere).

**Carbon sink**: a natural or manmade reservoir that accumulates and stores some carbon-containing chemical compound for an indefinite period.

**Climate change**: a change in the statistical distribution of weather over periods of time that range from decades to millions of years; it can be a change in average weather or a change in the distribution of weather events around an average (i.e. greater or fewer extreme weather events).

**Congener**: another organism within the same genus.

**Conspecific**: another organism within the same species.

**Consumer surplus value:** a measure of the personal satisfaction that people gain from the consumption of goods and services.

**El Niño:** a condition of decreased westward winds over the equatorial Pacific. This results in warm waters in the eastern Pacific that reduce nutrient availability, having significant consequences for coastal fisheries of western North and South America.

**Elevational range:** the component of a species range in terms of the elevation or altitude it occupies.

**Expenditure added value:** the economic impact of direct and indirect activities.

**Extratropical Cyclones:** a type of storm system formed in middle or high latitudes, in regions of large horizontal temperature variations called frontal zones; they present a contrast to the more violent cyclones or hurricanes of the tropics, which form in regions of relatively uniform temperatures.

**Forcing (climate):** altering the global energy balance and "forcing" the climate to change though mechanisms such as variations in ocean circulation and changes in the composition of the Earth's atmosphere, which can occur naturally or be human induced (i.e. through greenhouse gas emissions).

**Frontogenesis:** the formation or strengthening of an atmospheric front.

**Greenhouse gases:** naturally occurring gases in the atmosphere that absorb and emit radiation within the thermal infrared range to cause the "greenhouse effect;" without them the Earth would the about 59° F warmer than at present; the main gases are water vapor, carbon dioxide, methane, nitrous oxide, and ozone; since the start of the Industrial Revolution, human activities have increased the levels of greenhouse gases in the atmosphere.

**Heat shock protein (HSP):** molecular chaperone that modifies the shape and accumulation of other proteins.

**Hyper-nutrified:** a body of water containing high levels of nutrients such as nitrogen and phosphorus.

**Insolation:** a measure of solar radiation.

**Interannual** (time scale, variability): Variation that occurs predominantly between years.

**Interdecadal** (time scale, variability): Variation that occurs predominantly between decades.

**Keystone species:** a species that has a disproportionate effect on its environment relative to its biomass; such species affect many other organisms in an ecosystem and help determine the types and numbers of various other species in a community.

**La Niña:** a condition of unusually cold water temperatures in the tropical eastern Pacific, also the opposing condition to El Niño.

**Lithic:** referring to a stone tool.

**Macroalgae:** large aquatic photosynthetic plants that can been seen without the aid of a microscope.

**Marine layer:** an air mass that develops over a body of water and thus takes on the characteristics of both the moisture and temperature of the water. The air mass is trapped under a strong temperature inversion. Given that the marine layer is composed of very moist cool air, it can contain clouds either elevated off the surface, which are called marine stratus, or clouds interesting the ground, which can be called sea fog.

**Mesotidal:** two to four meters of tidal range; used to classify coasts based solely on tidal range without regard to any other variable.

**Microtidal:** less than two meters of tidal range; constitute the largest percentage of the world's coasts.

**North Pacific Gyre Oscillation (NPGO):** Describes fluctuations in sea surface height and temperature data across the northeastern Pacific in combination with the PDO; while the PDO is the dominant signal in physical parameters like temperature and sea level, the NPGO correlates well with salinity, nutrient concentrations and phytoplankton chlorophyll, suggesting a closer relationship to nutrient fluxes and ecosystem productivity.

**North Pacific High (NPH):** a semi-permanent, subtropical area of high pressure in the North Pacific Ocean; strongest in the Northern Hemispheric summer and displaced towards the equator during the winter when the Aleutian Low becomes more dominate.

**Oligotrophic:** an ecosystem or environment offering little to sustain life; commonly used to describe bodies of water or soils with very low nutrient levels.

**Pacific Decadal Oscillation (PDO):** a longer-term fluctuation in ocean climate that changes state approximately every 20-40 years.

**Palolo rising:** an annual mass spawning event that takes place in the Southern Hemisphere in October or November. The reproductive portion of the palolo worm (*Palola viridis*) is gathered with a net and eaten raw or cooked by people in the Samoan Islands.

**Phenology:** the study of periodic plant and animal life cycle events and how these are influenced by seasonal and interannual variations in climate.

**Population Connectivity:** the exchange of individuals between geographically isolated sub-populations through mechanisms such as larval dispersal or migration.

**Producer surplus value:** In economics the difference between the sale price and the production cost of a product.

**Return period:** the statistically estimated amount of time that will elapse before events.

**Saturation depth (horizon):** surface ocean waters are supersaturated with respect to $CaCO_3$ (calcite or aragonite), which becomes more soluble with decreasing temperature and increasing pressure (hence depth). A natural boundary, the saturation horizon develops when the saturation states falls under unity and $CaCO_3$ readily dissolves (http://www.co2.ulg.ac.be/peace/intro.htm).

**Saturation state:** the degree to which seawater is saturated with respect to carbonate minerals (e.g., calcite, aragonite, and high-magnesium calcites). Typically given as $\Omega$.

**Significant wave height ($H_s$):** the average height of the one third highest waves.

**Stratification:** the building up of layers.

**Stratus:** a cloud in the form of a gray layer with a rather uniform base. It seldom produces precipitation but if it does, it is in the form of drizzle. It is often seen in the summer months along the California coast. When this cloud comes in contact with the surface it is called fog.

**Stressor:** an agent, condition, or other stimulus that causes stress to an organism.

**Subsidence:** a descending motion of air in the atmosphere, usually with the implication that the condition extends over a broad area.

**Thermocline:** a thin but distinct layer in a large body of fluid (e.g., water, such as an ocean or lake, or air, such as an atmosphere), in which temperature changes more rapidly with depth than it does in the layers above or below; in the ocean, the thermocline may be thought of as an invisible blanket which separates the upper mixed layer from the calm deep water below.

**Top-down:** top predators are controlling the structure/population dynamics of the ecosystem.

**Turbulence:** the irregular or chaotic flow of a fluid (e.g., air or water).

**Uptake:** an act of taking in or absorbing.

**Upwelling:** results from the offshore transport of near-surface water due to alongshore winds from the north and the influence of the earth's rotation (known as Ekman transport), this water is replaced with cold, salty, nutrient-rich water from depths below.

**Wind curl (stress):** the drag or tangential force per unit area exerted on the surface of the earth by the adjacent layer of moving air.

**Wind shear:** a change in wind direction and speed between slightly different altitudes, especially a sudden downdraft.

**Zooxanthellae:** photosynthetic algae found in the tissue of most reef-building corals. Zooxanthellae supply the coral with glucose, glycerol and amino acids, which coral uses to make proteins, fats, and carbohydrates and produce calcium carbonate. In addition, zooxanthellae are responsible for the unique and beautiful colors of many stony corals.

# References

Aeby, G.S. 2007. First record of coralline lethal orange disease (CLOD) in the Northwestern Hawaiian Islands. *Coral Reefs* 26:385.

Addison, D., C.W. Filimoehala, S.J. Quintus, and T. Sapienza. 2010. Damage to Archaeological Sites on Tutuila Island (American Samoa) Following the 29 September 2009 Tsunami. *Rapa Nui Journal* 24:34-44.

Agegian, C.R. 1985. The biogeochemical ecology of *Porolithon gardineri* (Foslie). Ph.D. Dissertation. University of Hawaii.

Alory, G. and T. Delcroix. 1999. Climatic variability in the vicinity of Wallis, Futuna, and Samoa islands (13-15 S, 180-170 W). *Oceanologica Acta* 22:249-263.

Barnett, J. 2001. Adapting To Climate Change in Pacific Island Countries: The Problem of Uncertainty. *World Development* 29:977-993.

Barshis, D.J., J.H. Stillman, R.D. Gates, R.J. Toonen, L.W. Smith, and C. Birkeland. 2010. Protein expression and genetic structure of the coral *Porites lobata* in an environmentally extreme Samoan back reef: does host genotype limit phenotypic plasticity? *Molecular Ecology* 19:1705-1720.

Beardall J. and S. Stojkovic. 2006. Microalgae under Global Environmental Change: Implications for Growth and Productivity, Populations and Trophic flow. *Science Asia* 32 S1:1-10.

Bernal, P. A. 1993. Global climate change in the oceans: a review. In: Mooney, H.A., Fuentes, E.R. and Kronberg, B.I. (eds.), Earth System Responses to Global Change: Contrast between North and South America. Academic Press, San Diego, CA, pp. 1–15.

Berstein et al. 2007. *Summary for Policymakers*. Climate Change 2007: Synthesis Report by the Intergovernmental Panel on Climate Change. Available at: http://www.ipcc.ch/pdf/assessment-report/ar4/syr/ar4_syr_spm.pdf

Bessat, F. and D. Buigues. 2001. Two centuries of variation in coral growth in a massive *Porites* colony from Moorea (French Polynesia): A response of ocean-atmosphere variability from south central Pacific. *Palaeogeography Palaeoclimatology Palaeoecology* 175:381–392.

Bevelhimer, M. and W. Bennett. 2000. Assessing cumulative thermal stress in fish during chronic intermittent exposure to high temperatures. *Environment Science Policy* 3:S211–S216.

Bindoff, N., J. Willebrand, V. Artale, A. Cazenave, J. Gregory, S. Gulev, K. Hanawa, C. Le Quéré, S. Levitus, Y. Nojiri, C. Shum, L. Talley, and A. Unnikrishnan. Observations: Oceanic Climate Change and Sea Level. In: Solomon S, Qin D, Manning M, Chen Z, Marquis M, Averyt KB, Tignor M, Miller HL, editor. Climate Change 2007: The Physical Science Basis Contribution of Working Group I to the Fourth Assessment Report of the Intergovernmental Panel on Climate Change. Cambridge, United Kingdom and New York, NY, USA: Cambridge University Press; 2007. pp. 385–432.

Birkeland, C. 1982. Terrestrial runoff as a cause of outbreaks of *Acanthaster planci* (Echinodermata: Asteroidea). *Marine Biology* 69: 175-185.

Birkeland, C., R. Randall, R. Wass, B. Smith, and S. Wilkins. 1987. NOAA technical memoranda series NOS/MEMD: Biological Resource Assessment of the Fagatele Bay National Marine Sanctuary.

Birkeland, C., R. Randall, A. Green, B. Smith, and S. Wilkins. 2003. Changes in the coral reef communities of Fagatele Bay NMS and Tutuila Island (American Samoa), 1982-1995. Fagatele Bay National Marine Sanctuary Science Series. Pago Pago, AS. p. 237

Brainard R., and 25 others. 2008. Coral reef ecosystem monitoring report for American Samoa: 2002-2006. NOAA Special Report NMFS PIFSC. 472 pp.

Brandt, M.E. and J.W. McManus. 2009. Disease incidence is related to bleaching extent in reef-building corals. *Ecology* 90:2859-2867.

Brewer, P.G., T. Ohsumi, J. Ishizaka, J. Kita, and Y. Watanabe (special editors). 2004. Special Section on Ocean Sequestration of Carbon Dioxide. *Journal of Oceanography* 60:691– 816.

Brodie, J., Fabridius, K., De'ath, G., and K. Okaji. 2005. Are increased nutriet inputs responsible for more outbreaks of crown-of-thorns starfish? An appraisal of the evidence. *Marine Pollution Bulletin* 51: 266-278.

Brown, B. E. 1997. Coral bleaching: Causes and consequences. *Coral Reefs* 16:S129-S138.

Bumrungsri S. 2002. The foraging ecology of the short-nosed fruit bat, *Cynopterus brachyotis* (Muller, 1838), in lowland dry evergreen rain forest, Southeast Thailand. PhD dissertation, University of Aberdeen.

Caldeira K. and M.E. Wickett. 2003. Anthropogenic carbon and ocean pH. *Nature* 425:365.

Carricart-Ganivet, J.P. 2004. Sea surface temperature and the growth of the West Atlantic reef-building coral *Montastraea annularis*. *Journal of Experimental Marine Biology and* Ecology 302:249– 260.

Cazenave, A., and R.S. Nerem. 2004. Present-day sea level change: observations and causes. *Reviews of Geophysics* 42:RG3001

CCSP, 2008: *Weather and Climate Extremes in a Changing Climate*. Regions of Focus: North America, Hawaii, Caribbean, and U.S. Pacific Islands. A Report by the U.S. Climate Change Science Program and the Subcommittee on Global Change Research. [Thomas R. Karl, Gerald A. Meehl, Christopher D. Miller, Susan J. Hassol, Anne M. Waple, and William L. Murray (eds.)]. Department of Commerce, NOAA's National Climatic Data Center, Washington, D.C., USA, 164 pp.

Cecchini, S., Saroglia, M., Caricato, G., Terrova, G., and L. Sileo. 2001. Effects of graded environmental hypercapnia on sea bass (*Dicentrarchus labrax* L.) feed intake and acid-base balance. *Aquaculture Research* 32:499–502.

Cesar H., P. van Beukering, S. Pintz, and J. Dierking. 2002. Economic valuation of the coral reefs of Hawai' I (Final report). In Spurgeon, J., T. Roxburgh, S, O'Gorman, R. Lindley, D. Ramsey and N. Polunin. 2004. Economic Valuation of Coral Reefs and Adjacent Habitats in American Samoa. Jacobs.

Charles, M. (2005). Functions and socio-economic importance of coral reefs and lagoons and implications for sustainable management, vase study of Moorea, French Polynesia. Wageningen, Wageningen university, Master thesis, 147 p.

Chateau-Degat, M., M. Chinain, N. Cerf, S. Gingras, B. Hubert, and E. Dewailly. 2005. Seawater temperature, *Gambierdiscus* spp. variability and incidence of ciguatera poisoning in French Polynesia. *Harmful Algae* 4:1053–1062.

Chisholm, J. R. M., J. M. Jaubert, and G. Giaccone. 1995. *Caulerpa taxifolia* in the northwest Mediterranean: introduced species or migrant from the Red Sea? *Comptes Rendus de L'Academie des Sciences* 318:1219-1226.

Christiansen, S. "A fragile past: archaeologists are scrambling as accelerated erosion sweeps away artifacts on Alaska's Arctic coast." http://www.anchoragepress.com/articles/2010/05/19/news/doc4bf46dd8b550c180204 696.prt accessed October 10, 2010.

Church, J. and N. White. 2006. A 20th century acceleration in global sea-level rise. *Geophysical Research Letters* 33:L01602

Coles, S.L. and B.E. Brown. 2003. Coral bleaching - Capacity for acclimatization and adaptive selection. *Advances in Marine Biology* 46:183-224.

Coles, S.L., R.C. DeFelice, L.G. Eldredge and J.T. Carlton. 1997. Biodiversity of marine communities in Pearl Harbor, Oʻahu , Hawaiʻi with observations on introduced species. Techical Report No. 10, Bishop Museum, Honolulu.

Coles, S.L., R.C. DeFelice, L.G. Eldredge and J.T. Carlton. 1999a. Historical and recent introductions to non-indigenous marine species into Pearl Harbor, Oʻahu , Hawaiian Islands. *Marine Biology* 135:147-158.

Coles, S.L., R.C. DeFelice and L.G. Eldredge. 1999b. Nonindigenous marine species introductions in the harbors of the south and west shores of Oʻahu , Hawaiʻi. Tech. Rep. No. 15, Bishop Museum, Honolulu.

Coles S., P. Reath, P. Skelton, V. Bonito, R. DeFelice and L. Basch. 2003. Introduced marine species in Pago Pago harbor, Fagatele Bay and the National Park coast, American Samoa. Bishop Museum Technical Report No 26.

Costansa, R.et al. (1997) The value of the world's ecosystem services and natural capital, *Nature* 387, pp. 253-260.

Coutures, E. 2003. The Shoreline Fishery of American Samoa, analysis of 1-yr data and implementation of a new sampling protocol. Department of Marine and Wildlife Resources Report Series 102, Government of American Samoa. Pago Pago, American Samoa. 22pp.

Craig, P (editor). 2009. Natural history guide to American Samoa. 3rd Edition. National Park of American Samoa, Department of Marine and Wildlife Resources, and American Samoa Community College. Pago Pago, American Samoa. 131 pp.

Craig, P., C. Birkeland, and S. Belliveau. 2001. High temperatures tolerated by a diverse assemblage of shallow-water corals in American Samoa. *Coral Reefs* 20: 185-189.

Craig, P., P. Trail, and T.E. Morrell. 1994. The decline of fruit bats in American Samoa due to hurricanes and over hunting. *Biological Conservation* 69:261-266.

Curry, R., B. Dickson and I. Yashayaev. 2003. A change in the freshwater balance of the Atlantic Ocean over the past four decades. *Nature* 426:826–829.

Cushing, D.H. 1995. Population Production and Regulation in the Sea: a Fisheries Perspective Cambridge University Press, Cambridge.

Davenport, J. 1989. Sea turtles and the greenhouse effect. *British Herpetological Society Bulletin* 29:11-15.

Davenport, J. 1997. Temperature and the life-history strategies of sea turtles. *Journal of Thermal Biology* 22:479-488.

Department of Marine and Wildlife Resources. 2002. Web based documents including catch and effort data from the ongoing Creel Survey of commercial fish catches and descriptions of the various fisheries. In American Samoa in Spurgeon, J., T. Roxburgh, S, O'Gorman, R. Lindley, D. Ramsey and N. Polunin. 2004. Economic Valuation of Coral Reefs and Adjacent Habitats in American Samoa. Jacobs.

Department of Commerce (DOC). 2011. Department of Commerce, Statistics Division.

Domokos, R., M. P. Seki, J. J. Polovina and D. R. Hawn. 2007. Oceanographic investigation of the American Samoa albacore (*Thunnus alalunga*) habitat and longline fishing grounds. *Fisheries Oceanography* 16: 555-572.

Doney, S. C., V. J. Fabry, R. A. Feely, and J. A. Kleypas. 2009. Ocean acidification: The other $CO_2$ problem. *Annual Review of Marine Science* 1:169-192.

Dore, J.E., R. Lukas, D.W. Sadler, and D.M. Karl. 2003. Climate-driven changes to the atmospheric $CO_2$ sink in the subtropical North Pacific Ocean. *Nature* 424:754–757.

Douglas, B.C. 1992. Global sea level acceleration. *Journal of Geophysical Research* 97:12699–12706.

Dukes, J. S., H. Mooney. 1999. Does global change increase the success of biological invaders? *Trends in Ecology and Evolution* 14:135–139.

Easterling, D.R., G.A. Meehl, C. Parmesan, S.A. Chagnon, T.R. Karl, and L.O. Mearns. 2000. Climate extremes: Observations, modeling, and impacts. *Science* 289:2068-2074.

Edwards, M. and A. J. Richardson. 2004. Impact of climate change on marine pelagic phenology and trophic mismatch. *Nature* 430:881-884.

Emanuel, K. 2005. Increasing destructiveness of tropical cyclones over the past 30 years. *Nature* 436: 686-688.

Emanuel, K., R. Sundararajan, and J. Williams. 2008. Hurricanes and Global Warming: Results from downscaling IPCC AR4 simulations. *Bulletin of the American Meteorological Society* 89:347-367.

Fabry, V. J., B. A. Seibel, R. A. Feely, and J. C. Orr. 2008. Impacts of ocean acidification on marine fauna and ecosystem processes. *ICES Journal of Marine Science* 65:414-432.

Falkowski P., M. Katz, A. Knoll, A. Quigg, J. Raven, O. Schofield, F. Taylor. 2004. The Evolution of Modern Eukaryotic Phytoplankton. *Science* 305:354–360.

Fagatele Bay National Marine Sanctuary – Draft Management Plan/DEIS. 2011. *In prep.*

Federal Sunken Military Craft Act (H.R. 4200) 2005.

Feely, R. A., C. L. Sabine, K. Lee, W. Berelson, J. Kleypas, V. J. Fabry, and F. J. Millero. 2004. Impact of anthropogenic CO2 on the CaCO3 system in the oceans. *Science* 305:362-366.

Fenner, D., and S. Heron. 2009. Annual summer mass bleaching of a multi-species coral community in American Samoa. Proceedings of the 11th International Coral Reef Symposium, Ft. Lauderdale. 1289-1293. http://www.nova.edu/ncri/11icrs/proceedings/files/m25-04.pdf#zoom=100

Fenner, D., M. Speicher, S. Gulick, and 35 others. 2008. The State of Coral Reef Ecosystems of American Samoa. Pp. 307-351. In: The State of Coral Reef Ecosystems of the United States and Pacific Freely Associated States: 2008. Waddell,

J.E. and A.M. Clarke (eds.). NOAA Technical Memorandum NOS NCCOS 73. NOAA/NCCOS Center for Coastal Monitoring and Assessment. Biogeography Team. Silver Spring, MD. 569 pp.

Ferrier-Pagés, C., J.-P. Gattuso, S. Dallot, and J. Jaubert. 2000. Effect of nutrient enrichment on growth and photosynthesis of the zooxanthellate coral *Stylophora pistillata*. *Coral Reefs* 19:103–113.

Fine, M. and Y. Loya. 2003. Alternate coral-bryozoan competitive superiority during coral bleaching. *Marine Biology* 142:989–996.

Fisk, D. and C. Birkeland. 2002. Status of coral communities on the volcanic islands of American Samoa. Department of Marine and Wildlife Resources, Government of American Samoa. Pago Pago, American Samoa. 135 pp.

Fraga S. and A. Bakun. 1993. Climate change and harmful algal blooms: The example of *Gymnodinium catenatum* on the Galician Coast. In: Smayda TJ, Shimizu Y, editor. Toxic Phytoplankton Blooms in the Sea. New York: Elsevier Science Publishers;. pp. 59–65.

GAO-07-863. 2007. Climate Change: Agencies Should Develop Guidance for Addressing the Effects on Land and Water Resources. http://www.gao.gov/products/GAO-07-863

Gent, P.R. 2001. Will the North Atlantic Ocean thermohaline circulation weaken during the 21$^{st}$ century? *Geophysical Research Letters* 28:1023-1026.

Glynn, P.W. 1993. Coral reef bleaching: Ecological perspectives. *Coral Reefs* 12:1-17.

Glynn, P.W. and L. D'Croz. 1990. Experimental evidence for high temperature stress as the cause of El Niño coincident coral mortality. *Coral Reefs* 8: 181-191.

Godley, B.J., A.C. Broderick, F. Glen, G.C. Hays. 2002. Temperature-dependent sex determination of Ascension Island green turtles. *Marine Ecology Progress Series* 226:115-124.

Gonzalez-Dávila, M., et al. 2003. Seasonal and interannual variability of sea-surface carbon dioxide species at the European Station for Time Series in the Ocean at the Canary Islands (ESTOC) between 1996 and 2000. *Global Biogeochemical Cycles* 17:1076

Goreau, T.J. and R. Hayes. 1994. Survey of coral reef bleaching in the South Central Pacific during 1994: Report to the International Coral Reef Initiative. Global Coral Reef Alliance. Chappaqua, New York. 201 pp.

Goreau, T.J., et al. 1998. Rapid spread of diseases in Caribbean coral reefs. *Revista de Biologia Tropical* S46:157-171.

Green, M.A., M.E. Jones, C.L. Boudreau, R.L. Moore, and B.A. Westman. 2004. Dissolution mortality of juvenile bivalves in coastal marine deposits. *Limnology and Oceanography* 49:727–734.

Hales S., P. Weinstein and A. Woodward. 1999. Ciguatera (Fish Poisoning), El Niño, and Pacific Sea Surface Temperatures. *Ecosystem Health* 5:20–25.

Halpin, P. M., P. T. Strub, W. T. Peterson, and T. M. Baumgartner. 2004. An overview of interactions among oceanography, marine ecosystems, climatic and human disruptions along the eastern margins of the Pacific Ocean. *Revista Chilena de Historia Natural* 77: 371-409.

Hansen, B., S. Østerhus, D. Quadfasel, and W. Turrell. 2004. Already the day after tomorrow? *Science* 305:953–954.

Hallegraeff, G.M. 1993. A review of harmful algal blooms and their apparent global increase. *Phycologia* 32:79-99.

Harvell, C.D. et al. 2002. Climate warming and disease risks for terrestrial and marine biota. *Science* 296:2158.

Hayashi, M., J. Kita, and A. Ishimatsu. 2004. Acid-base responses to lethal aquatic hypercapnia in three marine fishes. *Marine Biology* 144:153–160.

Hayes, G.C., A.C. Broderick, F. Glen, and B.J. Godley. 2003. Climate change and sea turtles: a 150-year reconstruction of incubation temperatures at a major marine turtle rookery. *Global Change Biology* 9:642:646.

Heldtberg, M. and I.D. MacLeod and V.L. Richards. Corrosion and cathodic protection of iron in seawater: a case study of the *James Matthews* (1841). *Proceedings of Metal 2004* National Museum of Australia. Canberra ACT, 4-8 October, 2004.

Hester, K.C., E.T. Peltzer, W.J. Kirkwood, and P.G. Brewer. 2008. Unanticipated consequences of ocean acidification: A noisier ocean at lower pH. *Geophysical Research Letters* 35:L19601.

Hoegh-Guldberg, O., and G.J. Smith. 1989. Influence of the population density of zooxanthellae and supply of ammonium on the biomass and metabolic characteristics of the reef corals *Seriatopora hystrix* and *Stylophora pistillata*. *Marine Ecology Progress Series* 57:173–186.

Hoegh-Guldberg, O. 1999. Climate Change, coral bleaching and the future of the world's coral reefs. *Marine and Freshwater Research* 50:839-866.

Hughes, T.P., D.R. Bellwood, C. Folke, R.S. Steneck, and J. Wilson. 2005. New paradigms for supporting the resilience of marine ecosystems. *Trends in Ecology and Evolution*, 20(7), 380-386.

Hughes L. 2003. Climate change and Australia: trends, projections and impacts. *Austral Ecology* 28:423–443.

Iglesias-Rodriguez, M.D., P.R. Halloran, R.E.M. Rickaby, I.R. Hall, E. Colmenero-Hidalgo, J.R. Gittins, D.R.H. Green, T. Tyrrell, S.J. Gibbs, P. von Dassow, E. Rehm, E.V. Armbrust, and K.P. Boessenkool. 2008. Phytoplankton Calcification in a High-$CO_2$ World. *Science* 320:336-340.

Intergovernmental Panel on Climate Change, I. 2007. Climate Change 2007: The Scientific Basis. Working Group II Contribution to the Intergovernmental Panel on Climate Change Fourth Assessment Report.

Invers, O., R.C. Zimmerman, R.S. Alberte, M. Perez, and J. Romero. 2001. Inorganic carbon sources for seagrass photosynthesis: an experimental evaluation of bicarbonate use in species inhabiting temperate waters. *Journal of Experimental Marine Biology and Ecology* 265:203–217.

Invers, O., F. Tomas, M. Perez, and J. Romero. 2002. Potential effect of increased global $CO_2$ availability on the depth distribution of the seagrass *Posidonia oceanica* (L.) Delile: A tentative assessment using a carbon balance model. *Bulletin of Marine Science* 71:1191–1198.

Ishimatsu, A., Hayashi, M., and Lee, S. 2005. Physiological effects on fishes in a high-$CO_2$ world. *Journal of the American Geophysical Union* 110:C09S09.

Ishimatsu, A., Kikkawa, T., Hayashi, M., Lee, K., and Kita, J. 2004. Effects of $CO_2$ on marine fish: larvae and adults. *Journal of Oceanography* 60:731–741.

Jazen F.J. and G.L. Paukstis. 1991. Environmental sex determination in reptiles: ecology, evolution and experimental design. *Quarterly Review of Biology* 66:149-179.

Jokiel, P. L. 2004. Temperature stress and coral bleaching. pp. 401-425. *In:* E. Rosenberg & Y. Loya (ed.) Coral Health and Disease., Springer-Verlag, Heidelberg.

Kennedy, J. 2005. Results of an archaeological survey and archival research of WWII coastal defenses on Tutuila Island, American Samoa. Haleiwa, HI: Archaeological Consultants of the Pacific.

Kikkawa, T., A. Ishimatsu, and J. Kita. 2003. Acute $CO_2$ tolerance during the early developmental stages of four marine teleosts. *Environmental Toxicology* 18:375–382.

Kikkawa, T., J. Kita, and A. Ishimatsu. 2004. Comparison of the lethal effect of $CO_2$ and acidification on red sea bream (*Pagrus major*) during the early development stages. *Marine Pollution Bulletin* 48:108–110.

Kikkawa, T., Sata, T., Kita, J., and Ishimatsu, A. 2006. Acute toxicity of temporally varying seawater $CO_2$ conditions on juveniles of Japanese sillago (*Sillago japonica*). *Marine Pollution Bulletin* 52:621- 625.

Kleypas, J.A., R.A. Feely, V.J. Fabry, C. Langdon, C.L. Sabine, and L.L. Robbins. 2006. Impacts of Ocean Acidification on Coral Reefs and Other Marine Calcifiers: A Guide for Future Research, report of a workshop held 18–20 April 2005, St. Petersburg, FL, sponsored by NSF, NOAA, and the U.S. Geological Survey, 88 pp.

Kleypas, J.A.; R. W. Buddemeier, D. Archer, J. Gattuso, C. Langdon, and B.N. Opdyke. 1999. Geochemical consequences of increased atmospheric carbon dioxide on coral reefs. *Science* 284:118-120.

Kudela, R., G. Pitcher, T. Probyn, F. Figueiras, T. Moita, and V. Trainer. 2005. Harmful Algal Blooms in Coastal Upwelling Systems. *Oceanography* 18:184–197.

LaDochy S., P. Ramirez, and W. Patzert. 2007. Southern California upwelling: Is recent weakening a result of global warming? 19th Conference on Climate Variability and Change San Antonio, TX.

Lambeck, K. 2002. Sea-level change from mid-Holocene to recent time: An Australian example with global implications. In: Ice Sheets, Sea Level and the Dynamic Earth [Mitrovica, J.X., and B. L. A. Vermeersen (eds.)]. Geodynamics Series Vol. 29, American Geophysical Union, Washington, DC, doi:10.1029/029GD03. 33–50.

Landsea, C.W., W.M. Gray, and L.A. Avila. 1996. Downward trends in the frequency of intense Atlantic hurricanes during the past five decades. *Geophysical Research Letters* 23:1697-1700.

Langdon, C., and M.J. Atkinson. 2005. Effect of elevated pCO2 on photosynthesis and calcification of corals and interactions with seasonal change in temperature/irradiance and nutrient enrichment. *Journal of Geophysical Research* 110:C09S07

Langdon, C., W.S. Broecker, D.E. Hammond, E. Glenn, K. Fitzsimmons, S.G. Nelson, T.H. Peng, I. Hajdas and G. Bonani. 2003. Effect of elevated $CO_2$ on the community metabolism of an experimental coral reef. *Global Biogeochemical Cycles* 17:1011

Largier, J.L., B.S. Cheng, and K.D. Higgason, editors.2010. *Climate Change Impacts: Gulf of the Farallones and Cordell Bank National Marine Sanctuaries*. Report of a Joint Working Group of the Gulf of the Farallones and Cordell BankNational Marine Sanctuaries Advisory Councils. 121pp.

Larkin, N.K. and D.E. Harrison. 2005. Global seasonal temperature and precipitation anomalies during El Niño autumn and winter. *Geophysical Research Letters* 32:L16705.

Latif, M., E. Roeckner, U. Mikolajewicz, and R. Voss. 2000. Tropical stabilization of the thermohaline circulation in a greenhouse warming simulation. *Journal of Climate* 13:1809-1813.

Leuliette, E.W., R.S. Nerem, and G.T. Mitchum. 2004. Calibration of TOPEX/Poseidon and Jason altimeter data to construct a continuous record of mean sea level change. *Marine Geodesy* 27:79–94.

Levin, S. A. and J. Lubchenco. 2008. Resilience, Robustness, and Marine Ecosystem-based Management. *BioScience* 58:27–32.

Lirman, D. 2000. Fragmentation in the branching coral *Acropora palmata* (Lamarck): growth, survivorship, and reproduction of colonies and fragments. *Journal of Experimental Marine Biology and Ecology* 251:41–57.

Littler, M.M. and D.S. Littler. 1995. Impact of CLOD Pathogen on Pacific Coral Reefs. *Science* 267:1356-1360.

Loeb, V., V. Siegel, O. Holm-Hansen, R. Hewitt, W. Fraser, W. Trivelpiece, and S. Trivelpiece. 1997. Effects of sea-ice extent and krill or salp dominance on the Antarctic food web. *Nature* 387:897-900.

Lough, J.M. and D.J. Barnes. 1997. Several centuries of variation in skeletal extension, density and calcification in massive *Porites* colonies from the Great Barrier Reef: A proxy for seawater temperature and a background of variability against which to identify unnatural change. *Journal of Experimental Marine Biology and Ecology* 211:29–67.

Lough, J.M. and D.J. Barnes. 2000. Environmental controls on growth of the massive coral *Porites*. *Journal of Experimental Marine Biology and Ecology* 245:225–243.

Luick, J. 2000. Seasonal and interannual sea levels in the western Equatorial Pacific from Topex/Poseidon. *Journal of Climate* 13: 672-676.

Manabe, S., R. J. Stouffer, M. J. and Spelman. 1994. Response of a coupled ocean atmosphere model to increasing atmosphere carbon dioxide. *Ambio* 23:44–49.

Marshall P.A. and H.Z. Schuttenberg. 2006. A Reef Manager's Guide to Coral Bleaching. Great Barrier Reef Marine Park Authority, Australia (ISBN 1-876945-40-0)

Marubini, F., and M.J. Atkinson. 1999. Effects of lowered pH and elevated nitrate on coral calcification. *Marine Ecology Progress Series* 188:117–121.

Marubini, F., and P.S. Davies. 1996. Nitrate increases zooxanthellae population density and reduces skeletogenesis in corals. *Marine Biology* 127:319–328.

Matsuzawa, Y., K. Sato, W. Sakamoto, and K.A. Bjorndal. 2002. Seasonal fluctuations in sand temperature: effects on the incubation period and mortality of loggerhead sea turtle (*Caretta caretta*) pre-emergent hatchlings in Minabe, Japan. *Marine Biology* 140:639-646.

McClain, C. R., S. R. Signorini, and J. R. Christian. 2004. Subtropical gyre variability observed by ocean-color satellites. *Deep-Sea Research Part II*. 51: 281–301.

Meehi G., T. Stocker, W. Collins, P. Friedlingstein, A. Gaye, J. Gregory, A. Kitoh, R. Knutti, J. Murphy, A. Noda, S. Raper, I. Watterson, A. Weaver, and Z. Zhao. Global Climate Projections. In: Solomon S, Qin D, Manning M, Chen Z, Marquis M, Averyt

KB, Tignor M, Miller HL, editor. 2007. Climate Change 2007: The Physical Science Basis Contribution of Working Group I to the Fourth Assessment Report of the Intergovernmental Panel on Climate Change. Cambridge, United Kingdom and New York, NY, USA: Cambridge University Press. pp. 747–845.

Mendes, J.M. and J.D. Woodley. 2002. Effect of the 1995-1996 bleaching event on polyp tissue depth, growth, reproduction and skeletal band formation in *Montastrea annularis*. *Marine Ecology Progress Series* 235:93-102.

Merrill, J.T. 1989. Atmospheric long range transport to the Pacific Ocean. *Chemical Oceanography* 10: 15-50.

Michaelidis, B., C. Ouzounis, A. Paleras, and H.O. Pörtner. 2005. Effects of long-term moderate hypercapnia on acid-base balance and growth rate in marine mussels *Mytilus galloprovincialis*. *Marine Ecology Progress Series* 293:109–118.

Michaelidis, B., Spring, A., and Pörtner, H. O. 2007. Effects of long- term acclimation to environmental hypercapnia on extracellular acid-base status and metabolic capacity in Mediterranean fish *Sparus aurata*. *Marine Biology* 150:1417–1429.

Michalek-Wagner, K. and B. Willis. 2001. Impacts of bleaching on the soft coal *Lobophytum compactum*. I. Fecundity, fertilization and offspring viability. *Coral Reefs* 19:231–239.

Mitchell, W., J. Chittleborough, B. Ronai, and G.W. Lennon, 2001: Sea level rise in Australia and the Pacific. In: Pacific Islands Conference on Climate Change, Climate Variability and Sea Level Rise, National Tidal Facility Australia, Rarotonga, Cook Islands, 3-7 April 2000. Flinders Press, Adelaide, Australia, pp. 47–57.

Mora, C. and A.F. Ospína. 2001. Tolerance to high temperatures and potential impact of sea warming in reef fishes of Gorgona Island (tropical eastern Pacific). *Marine Biology* 139:756–769.

Mrosovsky, N. and C. Pieau. 1991. Transitional range of temperature pivotal temperatures and thermosensitive stages for sex determination in reptiles. *Amphibia-Reptilia* 12:169-180.

Muckelroy, K. 1978. Maritime Archaeology. Cambridge University Press, Cambridge, United Kingdom.

Munday, P.L. , D. L. Dixsona, J. M. Donelsona, G. P. Jonesa, M. S. Pratchetta, G. V. Devitsinac and K. B. Døvingd. 2009. Ocean acidification impairs olfactory discrimination and homing ability of a marine fish. *Proceedings of the National Academy of Sciences of the United States of America* 106:1848-1852.

Munday, P.L., J.M. Leis, J.M. Lough, C.B. Paris, M.J. Kingsford, M.L. Berumen, and J. Lambrechts. 2009. Climate change and coral reef connectivity. Coral Reefs DOI 10.1007/s00338-008-0461-9.

Nakamura, T. and R. van Woesik. 2001. Differential survival of corals during the 1998-bleaching event is partially explained by water-flow rates and passive diffusion. *Marine Ecology Progress Series* 212: 301-304.

Nehring, S. 1996. Establishment of thermophilic phytoplankton species in the North Sea: biological indicators of climatic changes? *ICES Journal of Marine Science* 55:818-823.

Nerem, R.S., et al. 1999. Variations in global mean sea level associated with the 1997-1998 ENSO event: Implications for measuring long term sea level change. *Geophysical Research Letters* 26:3005–3008.

Nieder, J., G. La Mesa, and M. Vacchi. 2000. Blenniidae along the Italian coasts of the Ligurian and the Tyrrhenian Sea: Community structure and new records of *Scartella cristata* for northern Italy. *Cybium* 24:359-369.

NOAA 2004. Annotated bibliography of coral reef literature. 2010. NOAA Coastal and Ocean Resource Economics Program http://marineeconomics.noaa.gov

NOAA Tides and Currents Department.

O'Connor, M. I., J. F. Bruno, S. D. Gaines, B. S. Halpern, S. E. Lester, B. P. Kinlan, and J. M. Weiss. 2007. Temperature control of larval dispersal and the implications for marine ecology, evolution, and conservation. *Proceedings of the National Academy of Sciences of the United States of America* 104:1266-1271.

Occhipinti-Ambrogi, A. 2007. Global change and marine communities: Alien species and climate change. *Marine Pollution Bulletin* 55:342-352.

Ocean Resource Economics Program http://marineeconomics.noaa.gov

Ogston, A.S. and M.E. Field. 2010. Predictions of Turbidity Due to Enhanced Sediment Resuspension Resulting from Sea-Level Rise on a Fringing Coral Reef: Evidence from Molokai, Hawaii. *Journal of Coastal Research* 26:1027-1037.

Omori, M., H. Fukami, H. Kobinata and M. Hatta. 2001. Significant drop of fertilization of *Acropora* corals in 1999: an after-effect of heavy coral bleaching? *Limnology and Oceanography* 46:704–706.

Orr J., V. Fabry, O. Aumont, L. Bopp, S. Doney, R. Feely, A. Gnanadesikan, N. Gruber, A. Ishida, F. Joos, R. Key, K. Lindsay, E. Maier-Reimer, R. Matear, P. Monfray, A. Mouchet, R. Najjar, G. Plattner, K. Rodgers, C. Sabine, J. Sarmiento, R. Schlitzer, R. Slater, I. Totterdell, M. Weirig, Y. Yamanaka, and A. Yool. 2005. Anthropogenic ocean acidification over the twenty-first century and its impact on calcifying organisms. *Nature* 437:681–686.

Overfield, Michael. "Corrosion on Deep Gulf Shipwrecks of World War II." Paper presented to the 2005 International Oil Spill Conference. http://www.iosc.org/papers/IOSC2005a377.pdf accessed October 13, 2010.

Palacios, S. L., and R. C. Zimmerman. 2007. Response of eelgrass *Zostera marina* to $CO_2$ enrichment: possible impacts of climate change and potential for remediation of coastal habitats. *Marine Ecology Progress Series* 344: 1–13.

Parmesan, C. 1996. Climate and species' range. *Science* 382:765-766.

Pastorok, R.A. and G.R. Bilyard. 1985. Effects of sewage pollution on coral reef communities. *Marine Ecology Progress Series* 21:175-189.

Pearson, Colin. 1988. Conservation of Marine Archaeological Objects. Butterworth-Heinemann, London; Boston.

Pelejero, C., E. Calvo, M.T. McCulloch, J.F. Marshall, M.K. Gagan, J.M. Lough and B.N. Opdyke. 2005. Preindustrial to modern interdecadal variability in coral reef pH. *Science* 309:2204–2207.

Penland, L., J. Kloulechad, D. Idip, and R. van Woesik. 2003. Coral spawning in the western Pacific Ocean is related to solar insolation: evidence of multiple spawning events in Palau. *Coral Reefs* 23:133-140.

Peter, C., G. DiDonato, D. Fenner, and C. Hawkins. 2005. The State of Reef Ecosystems of American Samoa. Pp. 312-337. In J. Waddell (ed.), The States of Coral Reef Ecosystems of the United States and Pacific Freely associated States.

Pfeffer, W., J. Harper and S. O'Neel. 2008. Kinematic Constraints on Glacier Contributions to 21st-Century Sea-Level Rise. *Science* 321:1340 – 1343.

Pirhalla, D., V. Ransi, M.S. Kendall, and D. Fenner. 2010. Oceanography of the Samoan Archipelago in Biogeographic Assessment of the Samoan Archipelago. M.S. Kendall (ed). NOAA technical report (in prep).

Planque, B. and T. Frédou. 1999. Temperature and the recruitment of Atlantic cod (*Gadus morhua*). *Canadian Journal of Fisheries Aquatic Sciences* 56:2069-2077.

Plattner, G. K., F. Joos, T. F. Stocker, and O. Marchal. 2001. Feedback mechanisms and sensitivities of ocean carbon uptake under global warming. *Tellus* 53:564–592.

Polovina, J. J. 1996. Decadal variation in the trans-Pacific migration of northern bluefin tuna (*Thunnus thynnus*) coherent with climate-induced change in prey abundance. *Fish Oceanography* 5:114-119.

Polovina, JJ, E Howell, and M Abecassis. 2008. Ocean's least productive waters are expanding. *Geophysical Research Letters*. 35:L03618.

Precht, W. and R. Aronson. 2004. Climate flickers and range shifts of reef corals. *Frontiers in Ecology and the Environment* 2: 307–314.

Qiu, B., and S. Chen. 2004. Seasonal modulations in the eddy field of the South Pacific Ocean. *Journal of Physical Oceanography* 34:1515-1527.

Randall, C. and A. Szmant. 2009. Elevated Temperature Affects Development, Survivorship, and Settlement of the Elkhorn Coral, *Acropora palmata* (Lamarck 1816). *Biological Bulletin* 217: 269-282.

Rasmussen, E.M. and J.M. Wallace. 1983. Meteorological aspects of the El Niño/Southern Oscillation. *Science* 222:1195-1202.

Raven J., K. Caldeira, H. Elderfield, O. Hoegh-Guldberg, P. Liss, U. Riebesell, J. Shepherd, C. Turley, and A. Watson. 2005. Ocean acidification due to increasing atmospheric carbon dioxide. London: The Royal Society

Reeder, L. A., T.C. Rick, and J.M. Erlandson. 2010. Our disappearing past: a GIS analysis of the vulnerability of coastal archaeological resources in California's Santa Barbara Channel region. *Journal of Coastal Conservation*. DOI: 10.1007/s11852-010-0131-2.

Rey, J. 2007. Ciguatera: Document ENY-741 (IN742). Entomology and Nematology Department, Florida Cooperative Extension Service, Institute of Food and Agricultural Sciences, University of Florida. Online at http://edis.ifas.ufl.edu.

Reynaud, S., N. Leclercq, S. Romaine-Lioud, C. Ferrier- Pagés, J. Jaubert, and J.P. Gattuso. 2003. Interacting effects of $CO_2$ partial pressure and temperature on photosynthesis and calcification in a scleractinian coral. *Global Change Biology* 9:1660–1668.

Richter, H.V. and G.S. Cumming. 2008. First application of satellite telemetry to track African straw-coloured fruit bat migration. *Journal of Zoology* 275:172-176.

Roberts H., P. Wilson and A. Lugp-Fernandez. 1992. Biological and geological responses to physical processes: examples from modern reef systems of the Caribbean-Atlantic region. *Continental Shelf Research* 12:809-834.

Robinson, M. H., C.R. Alexander, C.W. Jackson, C.P. McCabe, D. Crass. 2010. Threatened Archaeological, Historic, and Cultural Resources of the Georgia Coast: Identification, Prioritization and Management Using GIS Technology. *Geoarchaeology* 25:312-326.

Rodgers, B.A. 2004. The Archaeologist's Manual for Conservation. New York: Kluwer Academic/Plenum Publishers.

Rosenberg, E. and Y. Ben-Haim. 2002. Microbial diseases of corals and global warming. *Environmental Microbiology* 4: 318–326.

Sakai, K. 1998a. Delayed maturation in the colonial coral *Goniastrea aspera* (Scleractinia): Whole-colony mortality, colony growth and polyp egg production. *Researches on Population Ecology* 40:287–292.

Sakai, K. 1998b. Effect of colony size, polyp size, and budding mode on egg production in a colonial coral. *Biological Bulletin* 195:319–325.

Samoan Studies Institute. *Ua Tālā le Ta`ui (Untying the Bundles of Fine Mats).* Pago Pago: American Samoa Community College, 2009.

Sarmiento, J. L., T. M. C. Hughes, R. J. Stouffer and S. Manabe. 1998. Simulated response of the ocean carbon cycle to anthropogenic climate warming. *Nature* 393:245–249.

Saucerman, S. 1995. The Inshore Fishery of American Samoa. 1991 – 1994. Department of Marine and Wildlife Resources Report Series 55, Government of American Samoa. Pago Pago, American Samoa. 35pp.

Seibel, B. A., and P.J. Walsh. 2001. Potential impacts of $CO_2$ injection on deep-sea biota. *Science* 294:319–320.

Seibel, B. A., and P.J. Walsh. 2003. Biological impacts of deep-sea carbon dioxide injection inferred from indices of physiological performance. *Journal of Experimental Biology* 206:641–650.

Shirayama, Y. and H. Thornton. 2005. Effect of increased atmospheric $CO_2$ on shallow water marine benthos. *Journal of Geophysical Research* 110:C09S08

Simmonds, M. 2009. Report of the workshop on cetaceans and climate change. SC/61/Rep4 submitted to the 61st annual meeting of the Scientific Committee of the International Whaling Commission. Madeira, Portugal.

Smith, L. 2008. Fluctuating reef environments maintain coral resiliency. Dissertation, University of Hawai'i.

Smith, L. and C. Birkeland. 2003. Managing NPSA's Coral Reefs in the Face of Global Warming: Research Project Report for Year 1. Hawaii Coop Fishery Unit, UH, Manoa. 32 pp.

Smith, S.V. and R.W. Buddemeier. 1992. Global change and coral reef ecosystems. *Annual Review of Ecology and Systematics* 23:89-118.

Solomon, S., D. Qin, M. Manning, Z. Chen, M. Marquis, K.B. Averyt, M. Tignor and H.L. Miller (eds.). 2007. Contribution of Working Group I to the Fourth Assessment Report of the Intergovernmental Panel on Climate Change. Cambridge University Press, Cambridge, United Kingdom and New York, NY, USA.

Solomon, S., G. Plattner, R. Knutti, and P. Friedlingstein. 2009. Irreversible climate change due to carbon dioxide emissions. *Proceedings of the National Academy of the United States of America* 106:1704-1709.

Somero, G.N. 2010. The physiology of climate change: how potentials for acclimatization and genetic adaptation will determine 'winners' and 'losers'. *Journal of Experimental Biology* 213:912-920.

SPSLCMP (South Pacific Sea Level and Climate Monitoring Project). 2007. Pacific Country Report on Sea Level and Climate: Their Present State, Samoa. South Pacific

Sea Level and Climate Monitoring Project. http://www.bom.gov.au/pacificsealevel/ 36 pp.

Spurgeon, J., T. Roxburgh, S, O'Gorman, R. Lindley, D. Ramsey and N. Polunin. 2004. Economic Valuation of Coral Reefs and Adjacent Habitats in American Samoa. Jacobs.

Stachowicz, J.J., J.R. Terwin, R.B. Whitlatch and R.W. Osman. 2002. Linking climate change and biological invasions: ocean warming facilitates non-indigenous species invasion. *Proceedings of the National Academy of Sciences of the United States of America* 99:15497–15500.

Stambler, N., N. Popper, Z. Dubinsky, and J. Stimson. 1991. Effect of nutrient enrichment and water motion on the coral *Pocillopora damicornis. Pacific Science* 45: 299–307.

Stillman, J. H. 2003. Acclimation capacity underlies susceptibility to climate change. *Science* 301:65-65.

Strutton, P. G., J. P. Ryan, and F. P. Chaves. 2001. Enhanced chlorophyll associated with tropical instability waves in the equatorial Pacific. *Geophysical Research Letters* 28: 2005-2008.

Suphachalasai, S. 2010. The Economics of Climate Change in the Pacific: Overview, Framework and Preliminary Findings. Powerpoint Presentation. Nadi, Fiji.

Szmant, A. M. and N. J. Gassman. 1990. The effects of prolonged "bleaching" on the tissue biomass and reproduction of the reef coral *Montastrea annularis. Coral Reefs* 8:217–224.

Tester, P. 1994. Harmful Marine Phytoplankton and Shellfish Toxicity: Potential Consequences of Climate Change. *Annals of the New York Academy of Sciences* 740:69–76.

Timmermann, A., J. Oberhuber, A. Bacher, M. Esch, M. Latif, and E. Roeckner. 1999. Increased El Niño frequency in a climate model forced by future greenhouse warming. *Nature* 398:694–696.

Tomczak, M. and J.S. Godfrey. 2003. Regional Oceanography: an Introduction. 2nd improved edition. Daya Publishing House, Delhi. 390p.

Truchot, J.P. 1987. Comparative aspects of extracellular acid-base balance. Berlin, New York. Springer-Verlag 248p.

University of Gothenburg. "Shipworm Threatens Archaeological Treasures." http://www.physorg.com/news182431980.html accessed October 10, 2010.

US EPA (United Stated Environmental Protection Agency). 2007. Climate Change and Interacting Stressors: Implications for Coral Reef Management in American Samoa. Global Change Research Program, National Center for Environmental Assessment, Washington DC; EPA/600/R-07/069 http://www.epa.gov/ncea. 61 pp.

van Oldenborgh, G.J., S.Y. Philip, and M. Collins. 2005. El Niño in a changing climate: a multi-model study. *Ocean Science* 1:81-95.

van Tilburg, H. 2007. American Samoa Maritime Heritage Inventory. Report to NOAA Office of National Marine Sanctuaries.

Vellinga, M. and R. A. Wood. 2002. Global climatic impacts of a collapse of the Atlantic thermohaline circulation. *Climate Change* 54:251–267.

Vitousek, P.M., H.A. Mooney, J. Lubchenco, and J.M. Melillo. 1997. Human Domination of Earth's Ecosystems. *Science* 277:494-499.

Volk, R.D., P.A. Knudsen, K.D. Kluge, and D.J. Herdrich. 1992. Towards a Territorial Conservation Strategy and the Establishment of a Conservation Areas System in American Samoa. Pago Pago: Le Vaumatua Inc.

Ward, M.N. and B.J. Hoskins. 1996. Near-surface wind over the Global Ocean 1949-1988. *Journal of Climate* 9-1877-1895.

Ward, S., P. Harrison, and O. Hoegh-Guldberg. 2000. Coral bleaching reduces reproduction of scleractinian corals and increases susceptibility to future stress. Proceedings 9th International Coral Reef Symposium, Bali, Indonesia 23-27 October 2000. 2:1123–1128.

Wass R. 1980. The Shoreline Fishery of American Samoa – Past and Present. American Samoa, USA.

Webster, P.J., G.J. Holland, J.A. Curry, H.R. Chang. 2005. Changes in Tropical Cyclone Number, Duration, and Intensity in a Warming Environment. *Science* 309:1844-1846.

Welbergen JA, Klose SM, Markus N, Eby P. 2008. Climate change and the effects of temperature extremes on Australian flying-foxes. *Proceedings of the Royal Society B* 275:419–425.

Wespestad, V., Fritz, L. W., Ingraham, J. W. and Megrey, B. A. 2000. On the relationship between cannibalism, climate variability, physical transport, and recruitment of Bering sea walleye pollock (*Theragra chalcogramma*). *ICES Journal of Marine Science* 57:272-278.

West, J., R. Salm. 2003 Resistance and resilience to coral bleaching: implications for coral Reef conservation and management. *Conservation Biology* 17:956-967.

WHO. Regional Office for the Western Pacific. Climate Change Country Profile: Samoa. Persistent link: www.wpro.who.int/NR/rdonlyres/8A552D76-8C7A-4278-AD5B-0AD730D5C80E/0/SMA.pdf Accessed April, 2010.

Williams, E. H., Jr.; L. Bunkley-Williams. 1990. The world-wide coral reef bleaching cycle and related sources of coral mortality. *Atoll Research Bulletin* 335:1-71.

Wong, A. P. S., N. L. Bindoff, and J. A. Church. 2001. Freshwater and heat changes in the North and South Pacific Oceans between the 1960s and 1985-94. *Journal of Climate* 14:1613–1633.

Wongbusarakum, S. 1997. Climate-Related Socioeconomic Assessment in American Samoa.

World Bank. 2010. *Economics of Adaptation to Climate Change: Samoa.* Washington DC: The World Bank.

Yeh, S., J. Kug, B. Dewitte, M. Kwon, B.P. Kirtman, and F. Jin. 2009. El Niño in a changing climate. *Nature* 461:511-515.

Young, W.J. 2007. Climate Risk Profile for Samoa. Samoa Meteorology Division. www.mnre.gov.ws/.../**climate**/.../**Samoa**%20CRP%20Updated%20ver%202007%20Final.pdf

Young, I.R., S. Zieger, and A.V. Babanin. 2011. *Global Trends in Wind Speed and Wave Height. Science 332:451-455.*

Zimmerman, R.C., D.G. Kohrs, D.L. Steller, and R.S. Alberte. 1997. Impacts of $CO_2$ enrichment on productivity and light requirements of eelgrass. *Plant Physiology* 115:599– 607.